Criminal Procedures

2018 Supplement

EDITORIAL ADVISORS

2018 Supplement

Criminal Procedures

Cases, Statutes, and Executive Materials

Fifth Edition

Marc L. Miller
Dean and Ralph W. Bilby Professor of Law
James E. Rogers College of Law, University of Arizona

Ronald F. Wright
Needham Y. Gulley Professor of Criminal Law
Wake Forest University School of Law

Jenia I. Turner
Amy Abboud Ware Centennial Professor in Criminal Law
Southern Methodist University, Dedman School of Law

Kay L. Levine
Professor of Law and Associate Dean of Faculty
Emory University School of Law

Published by Wolters Kluwer in New York.

Wolters Kluwer Legal & Regulatory U.S. serves customers worldwide with CCH, Aspen Publishers, and Kluwer Law International products. (www.WKLegaledu.com)

To contact Customer Service, e-mail customer.service@wolterskluwer.com, call 1-800-234-1660, fax 1-800-901-9075, or mail correspondence to:

Wolters Kluwer
Attn: Order Department
PO Box 990
Frederick, MD 21705

Printed in the United States of America.

1 2 3 4 5 6 7 8 9 0

ISBN 978-1-4548-9474-2

About Wolters Kluwer Legal & Regulatory U.S.

Wolters Kluwer Legal & Regulatory U.S. delivers expert content and solutions in the areas of law, corporate compliance, health compliance, reimbursement, and legal education. Its practical solutions help customers successfully navigate the demands of a changing environment to drive their daily activities, enhance decision quality and inspire confident outcomes.

Serving customers worldwide, its legal and regulatory portfolio includes products under the Aspen Publishers, CCH Incorporated, Kluwer Law International, ftwilliam.com and MediRegs names. They are regarded as exceptional and trusted resources for general legal and practice-specific knowledge, compliance and risk management, dynamic workflow solutions, and expert commentary.

Contents

20
Appeals 189

Preface

One function of a casebook supplement is to keep teachers and students current with recent events. In terms of basic doctrine, most aspects of criminal procedure have changed only modestly over the past few years. This is particularly true for a book, such as this one, that emphasizes nationwide trends within state criminal justice systems. Such nationwide changes can take longer to develop than any shifts in a single jurisdiction.

Nevertheless, these are remarkable times in criminal justice, and dramatic—even historic—events and major trends force their way into every vibrant criminal procedure course. One trend that has been building over the past few decades is a serious debate in many (but not all) states over the exceptional criminal sanctions we use in the United States, especially the historically high use of imprisonment and parole. On the other side of the scale, a decades-long decline in crime rates across the United States has shown preliminary and scattered signs of a reversal. In the federal system, Attorney General Sessions announced new policies designed to intensify the use of prisons. What has made punishment reform suddenly relevant? How important is leadership to such change?

Tragic police-involved shootings—leading to the deaths of Tamir Rice (age 12) in Ohio, Philando Castile in Minnesota, and Keith Scott in North Carolina—create astonishing news coverage, often with video footage. These events are so raw, so immediate, and so unpredictable that the full impact on the criminal justice system will not be known for some time. As just one example, an emerging trend towards the use of body-worn cameras by police officers throughout the country has become a camera tsunami, flooding tens of thousands of additional cameras into hundreds of law enforcement agencies. The push for cameras often comes without a clear articulation of what proponents hope body-worn cameras will achieve, much less a full understanding of the implications for privacy and the challenges of implementation. To what extent will cameras solve, sidestep, or even exacerbate underlying tensions in the evolving relationship of citizens and police?

Some of the materials in this supplement will appear in the next edition; other materials may eventually disappear from the print format materials and move to the web site. Many decisions from the U.S. Supreme Court seem on a first reading to make a dramatic shift in law and practice. However, after a year or two for reflection, some of those cases appear to be less important, because they merely restate or apply established concepts. A casebook supplement is a good opportunity to test the staying power of new cases, statutes, and policies.

This supplement is consistent with our larger goal of creating materials to extend the breadth and depth of the core casebook. We have also created internet-based pages for this casebook to enrich the resources available for students using this casebook. Our goal is not to create a single electronic coursebook. Instead, the electronic resources create different layers that broaden, deepen, and enliven the core text.

The *Criminal Procedures* web pages include materials allowing students to test and expand their knowledge, such as practice problems, exams, short excerpts of articles on criminal procedure, and "extension" topics to develop themes and sub-topics that receive passing attention in the printed text. They also include brief recorded lectures, or "video introductions," connected to selected materials in the printed text. The address for these pages is http://www.crimpro.com (or simply type "crimpro" into your browser). We welcome suggestions for materials to post on the web pages or to publish in this printed supplement.

We hope you find that the casebook, this supplement, and the web pages—together—offer a complete, coherent, and challenging set of tools for learning about criminal procedure.

Marc Miller
Ron Wright
Jenia Turner
Kay Levine

July 2018

Table of Cases

Principal cases are in italic.
Principal Supreme Court cases are in bold.

Chapter 2

Brief Searches and Stops

A. *Brief Investigative Stops of Suspects*

2. Grounds for Stops: Articulable, Individualized Reasonable Suspicion

Page 61. Add the following material before the Notes.

Nicholas Brady Heien v. North Carolina
135 S. Ct. 530 (2014)

ROBERTS, C.J.*

The Fourth Amendment prohibits "unreasonable searches and seizures." Under this standard, a search or seizure may be permissible even though the justification for the action includes a reasonable factual mistake. An officer might, for example, stop a motorist for traveling alone in a high-occupancy vehicle lane, only to discover upon approaching the car that two children are slumped over asleep in the back seat. The driver has not violated the law, but neither has the officer

---

[*Justices Scalia, Kennedy, Thomas, Ginsburg, Breyer, Alito, and Kagan joined this opinion—EDS.]

violated the Fourth Amendment.

But what if the police officer's reasonable mistake is not one of fact but of law? In this case, an officer stopped a vehicle because one of its two brake lights was out, but a court later determined that a single working brake light was all the law required. The question presented is whether such a mistake of law can nonetheless give rise to the reasonable suspicion necessary to uphold the seizure under the Fourth Amendment. We hold that it can. Because the officer's mistake about the brake-light law was reasonable, the stop in this case was lawful under the Fourth Amendment.

On the morning of April 29, 2009, Sergeant Matt Darisse of the Surry County Sheriff's Department sat in his patrol car near Dobson, North Carolina, observing northbound traffic on Interstate 77. Shortly before 8 A.M., a Ford Escort passed by. Darisse thought the driver looked "very stiff and nervous," so he pulled onto the interstate and began following the Escort. A few miles down the road, the Escort braked as it approached a slower vehicle, but only the left brake light came on. Noting the faulty right brake light, Darisse activated his vehicle's lights and pulled the Escort over.

Two men were in the car: Maynor Javier Vasquez sat behind the wheel, and petitioner Nicholas Brady Heien lay across the rear seat. Sergeant Darisse explained to Vasquez that as long as his license and registration checked out, he would receive only a warning ticket for the broken brake light. A records check revealed no problems with the documents, and Darisse gave Vasquez the warning ticket. But Darisse had become suspicious during the course of the stop—Vasquez appeared nervous, Heien remained lying down the entire time, and the two gave inconsistent answers about their destination. Darisse asked Vasquez if he would be willing to answer some questions. Vasquez assented, and Darisse asked whether the men were transporting various types of contraband. Told no, Darisse asked whether he could search the Escort. Vasquez said he had no objection, but told Darisse he should ask Heien, because Heien owned the car. Heien gave his consent, and Darisse, aided by a fellow officer who had since arrived, began a thorough search of the vehicle. In the side compartment of a duffle bag, Darisse found a sandwich bag containing cocaine. The officers arrested both men.

The State charged Heien with attempted trafficking in cocaine. Heien moved to suppress the evidence seized from the car, contending that the stop and search had violated the Fourth Amendment of the

United States Constitution. After a hearing at which both officers testified and the State played a video recording of the stop, the trial court denied the suppression motion, concluding that the faulty brake light had given Sergeant Darisse reasonable suspicion to initiate the stop, and that Heien's subsequent consent to the search was valid. Heien pleaded guilty but reserved his right to appeal the suppression decision.

The North Carolina Court of Appeals reversed. The initial stop was not valid, the court held, because driving with only one working brake light was not actually a violation of North Carolina law. The relevant provision of the vehicle code provides that a car must be

> equipped with a stop lamp on the rear of the vehicle. The stop lamp shall display a red or amber light visible from a distance of not less than 100 feet to the rear in normal sunlight, and shall be actuated upon application of the service (foot) brake. The stop lamp may be incorporated into a unit with one or more other rear lamps. N.C. Gen. Stat. § 20-129(g) (2007).

Focusing on the statute's references to "a stop lamp" and "the stop lamp" in the singular, the court concluded that a vehicle is required to have only one working brake light—which Heien's vehicle indisputably did. The justification for the stop was therefore "objectively unreasonable." . . .

The State appealed, and the North Carolina Supreme Court reversed. Noting that the State had chosen not to seek review of the Court of Appeals' interpretation of the vehicle code, the North Carolina Supreme Court assumed for purposes of its decision that the faulty brake light was not a violation. But the court concluded that, for several reasons, Sergeant Darisse could have reasonably, even if mistakenly, read the vehicle code to require that both brake lights be in good working order. Most notably, a nearby code provision requires that "all originally equipped rear lamps" be functional. Because Sergeant Darisse's mistaken understanding of the vehicle code was reasonable, the stop was valid. "An officer may make a mistake, including a mistake of law, yet still act reasonably under the circumstances. [When] an officer acts reasonably under the circumstances, he is not violating the Fourth Amendment." . . .

A traffic stop for a suspected violation of law is a "seizure" of the occupants of the vehicle and therefore must be conducted in accordance with the Fourth Amendment. All parties agree that to justify this type of

seizure, officers need only "reasonable suspicion"—that is, "a particularized and objective basis for suspecting the particular person stopped" of breaking the law. The question here is whether reasonable suspicion can rest on a mistaken understanding of the scope of a legal prohibition. We hold that it can.

As the text indicates and we have repeatedly affirmed, the ultimate touchstone of the Fourth Amendment is "reasonableness." To be reasonable is not to be perfect, and so the Fourth Amendment allows for some mistakes on the part of government officials, giving them "fair leeway for enforcing the law in the community's protection." We have recognized that searches and seizures based on mistakes of fact can be reasonable. The warrantless search of a home, for instance, is reasonable if undertaken with the consent of a resident, and remains lawful when officers obtain the consent of someone who reasonably appears to be but is not in fact a resident. By the same token, if officers with probable cause to arrest a suspect mistakenly arrest an individual matching the suspect's description, neither the seizure nor an accompanying search of the arrestee would be unlawful. The limit is that "the mistakes must be those of reasonable men."

But reasonable men make mistakes of law, too, and such mistakes are no less compatible with the concept of reasonable suspicion. Reasonable suspicion arises from the combination of an officer's understanding of the facts and his understanding of the relevant law. The officer may be reasonably mistaken on either ground. Whether the facts turn out to be not what was thought, or the law turns out to be not what was thought, the result is the same: the facts are outside the scope of the law. There is no reason, under the text of the Fourth Amendment or our precedents, why this same result should be acceptable when reached by way of a reasonable mistake of fact, but not when reached by way of a similarly reasonable mistake of law. . . .

Cases dating back two centuries support treating legal and factual errors alike in this context. Customs statutes enacted by Congress not long after the founding authorized courts to issue certificates indemnifying customs officers against damages suits premised on unlawful seizures. Courts were to issue such certificates on a showing that the officer had "reasonable cause"—a synonym for "probable cause"—for the challenged seizure. In United States v. Riddle, 3 L.Ed. 110 (1809), a customs officer seized goods on the ground that the English shipper had violated the customs laws by preparing an invoice

that undervalued the merchandise, even though the American consignee declared the true value to the customs collector. Chief Justice Marshall held that there had been no violation of the customs law because, whatever the shipper's intention, the consignee had not actually attempted to defraud the Government. Nevertheless, because "the construction of the law was liable to some question," he affirmed the issuance of a certificate of probable cause: "A doubt as to the true construction of the *law* is as reasonable a cause for seizure as a doubt respecting the fact."

This holding—that reasonable mistakes of law, like those of fact, would justify certificates of probable cause—was reiterated in a number of 19th-century decisions. By the Civil War, there had been "numerous cases in which [a] captured vessel was in no fault, and had not, under a true construction of the law, presented even ground of suspicion, and yet the captor was exonerated because he acted under an honest mistake of the law."

Riddle and its progeny are not directly on point. Chief Justice Marshall was not construing the Fourth Amendment, and a certificate of probable cause functioned much like a modern-day finding of qualified immunity, which depends on an inquiry distinct from whether an officer has committed a constitutional violation. But Chief Justice Marshall was nevertheless explaining the concept of probable cause, which, he noted elsewhere, "in all cases of seizure, has a fixed and well known meaning. It imports a seizure made under circumstances which warrant suspicion." We have said the phrase "probable cause" bore this "fixed and well known meaning" in the Fourth Amendment, and *Riddle* illustrates that it encompassed suspicion based on reasonable mistakes of both fact and law. No decision of this Court in the two centuries since has undermined that understanding.

The contrary conclusion would be hard to reconcile with a much more recent precedent. In Michigan v. DeFillippo, 443 U.S. 31 (1979), we addressed the validity of an arrest made under a criminal law later declared unconstitutional. A Detroit ordinance that authorized police officers to stop and question individuals suspected of criminal activity also made it an offense for such an individual "to refuse to identify himself and produce evidence of his identity." Detroit police officers sent to investigate a report of public intoxication arrested Gary DeFillippo after he failed to identify himself. A search incident to arrest uncovered drugs, and DeFillippo was charged with possession of a controlled substance. The Michigan Court of Appeals ordered the suppression of the drugs, concluding that the identification ordinance was unconstitutionally vague and that DeFillippo's arrest was therefore invalid.

Accepting the unconstitutionality of the ordinance as a given, we nonetheless reversed. At the time the officers arrested DeFillippo, we explained, "there was no controlling precedent that this ordinance was or was not constitutional, and hence the conduct observed violated a presumptively valid ordinance." Acknowledging that the outcome might have been different had the ordinance been "grossly and flagrantly unconstitutional," we concluded that under the circumstances "there was abundant probable cause to satisfy the constitutional prerequisite for an arrest."

The officers were wrong in concluding that DeFillippo was guilty of a criminal offense when he declined to identify himself. That a court only *later* declared the ordinance unconstitutional does not change the fact that DeFillippo's conduct was lawful when the officers observed it. But the officers' assumption that the law was valid was reasonable, and their observations gave them "abundant probable cause" to arrest DeFillippo. Although DeFillippo could not be prosecuted under the identification ordinance, the search that turned up the drugs was constitutional. . . .

Heien is correct that in a number of decisions we have looked to the reasonableness of an officer's legal error in the course of considering the appropriate remedy for a constitutional violation, instead of whether there was a violation at all. In those cases, however, we had already found or assumed a Fourth Amendment violation. An officer's mistaken view that the conduct at issue did *not* give rise to such a violation—no matter how reasonable—could not change that ultimate conclusion. Any consideration of the reasonableness of an officer's mistake was therefore limited to the separate matter of remedy.

Here, by contrast, the mistake of law relates to the antecedent question of whether it was reasonable for an officer to suspect that the defendant's conduct was illegal. If so, there was no violation of the Fourth Amendment in the first place. . . .

Heien also contends that the reasons the Fourth Amendment allows some errors of fact do not extend to errors of law. Officers in the field must make factual assessments on the fly, Heien notes, and so deserve a margin of error. In Heien's view, no such margin is appropriate for questions of law: The statute here either requires one working brake light or two, and the answer does not turn on anything "an officer might suddenly confront in the field." But Heien's point does not consider the reality that an officer may "suddenly confront" a situation in the field as to which the application of a statute is unclear—however clear it may later become. A law prohibiting "vehicles" in the park either covers Segways or not, but an officer will nevertheless have to make a quick decision on the law the first time one whizzes by.

Contrary to the suggestion of Heien and *amici,* our decision does not discourage officers from learning the law. The Fourth Amendment tolerates only *reasonable* mistakes, and those mistakes—whether of fact or of law—must be *objectively* reasonable. We do not examine the subjective understanding of the particular officer involved. And the inquiry is not as forgiving as the one employed in the distinct context of deciding whether an officer is entitled to qualified immunity for a constitutional or statutory violation. Thus, an officer can gain no Fourth Amendment advantage through a sloppy study of the laws he is duty-bound to enforce.

Finally, Heien and *amici* point to the well-known maxim, "Ignorance of the law is no excuse," and contend that it is fundamentally unfair to let police officers get away with mistakes of law when the citizenry is accorded no such leeway. Though this argument has a certain rhetorical appeal, it misconceives the implication of the maxim. The true symmetry is this: Just as an individual generally cannot escape criminal liability based on a mistaken understanding of the law, so too the government cannot impose criminal liability based on a mistaken understanding of the law. If the law required two working brake lights, Heien could not escape a ticket by claiming he reasonably thought he needed only one; if the law required only one, Sergeant Darisse could not issue a valid ticket by claiming he reasonably thought drivers needed two. But just because mistakes of law cannot justify either the imposition or the avoidance of criminal liability, it does not follow that they cannot justify an investigatory stop. And Heien is not appealing a brake-light ticket; he is appealing a cocaine-trafficking conviction as to which there is no asserted mistake of fact or law. . . .

Here we have little difficulty concluding that the officer's error of law was reasonable. Although the North Carolina statute at issue refers to "*a* stop lamp," suggesting the need for only a single working brake light, it also provides that "the stop lamp may be incorporated into a unit with one or more *other* rear lamps." N.C. Gen. Stat. § 20-129(g) (emphasis added). The use of "other" suggests to the everyday reader of English that a "stop lamp" is a type of "rear lamp." And another subsection of the same provision requires that vehicles "have all originally equipped rear lamps or the equivalent in good working order," arguably indicating that if a vehicle has multiple "stop lamps," all must be functional.

The North Carolina Court of Appeals concluded that the "rear lamps" discussed in subsection (d) do not include brake lights, but, given the "other," it would at least have been reasonable to think they did. Both the majority and the dissent in the North Carolina Supreme Court so concluded, and we agree. This "stop lamp" provision, moreover, had never been previously construed by North Carolina's appellate courts. It was thus objectively reasonable for an officer in Sergeant Darisse's position to think that Heien's faulty right brake light was a violation of North Carolina law. And because the mistake of law was reasonable, there was reasonable suspicion justifying the stop. . . .

SOTOMAYOR, J., dissenting.

The Court is, of course, correct that the ultimate touchstone of the Fourth Amendment is "reasonableness." But this broad statement simply sets the standard a court is to apply when it conducts its inquiry into whether the Fourth Amendment has been violated. It does not define the categories of inputs that courts are to consider when assessing the reasonableness of a search or seizure, each of which must be independently justified. What this case requires us to decide is whether a police officer's understanding of the law is an input into the reasonableness inquiry, or whether this inquiry instead takes the law as a given and assesses an officer's understanding of the facts against a fixed legal yardstick.

I would hold that determining whether a search or seizure is reasonable requires evaluating an officer's understanding of the facts against the actual state of the law. I would accordingly reverse the judgment of the North Carolina Supreme Court, and I respectfully dissent from the Court's contrary holding.

[The] leeway we afford officers' factual assessments is rooted not only in our recognition that police officers operating in the field have to make quick decisions, but also in our understanding that police officers have the expertise to draw inferences and make deductions "that might well elude an untrained person." When officers evaluate unfolding circumstances, they deploy that expertise to draw conclusions about human behavior much in the way that jurors do *as factfinders*.

The same cannot be said about legal exegesis. After all, the meaning of the law is not probabilistic in the same way that factual determinations are. Rather, the notion that the law is definite and knowable sits at the foundation of our legal system. And it is courts, not officers, that are in the best position to interpret the laws.

Both our enunciation of the reasonableness inquiry and our justification for it thus have always turned on an officer's factual conclusions and an officer's expertise with respect to those factual conclusions. Neither has hinted at taking into account an officer's understanding of the law, reasonable or otherwise.

[Permitting] mistakes of law to justify seizures has the perverse effect of preventing or delaying the clarification of the law. Under such an approach, courts need not interpret statutory language but can instead simply decide whether an officer's interpretation was reasonable. Indeed, had this very case arisen after the North Carolina Supreme Court announced its rule, the North Carolina Court of Appeals would not have had the occasion to interpret the statute at issue. . . . This result is bad for citizens, who need to know their rights and responsibilities, and it is bad for police, who would benefit from clearer direction.

Of course, if the law enforcement system could not function without permitting mistakes of law to justify seizures, one could at least argue that permitting as much is a necessary evil. But I have not seen any persuasive argument that law enforcement will be unduly hampered by a rule that precludes consideration of mistakes of law in the reasonableness inquiry. After all, there is no indication that excluding an officer's mistake of law from the reasonableness inquiry has created a problem for law enforcement in the overwhelming number of Circuits which have adopted that approach. If an officer makes a stop in good faith but it turns out that, as in this case, the officer was wrong about what the law proscribed or required, I know of no penalty that the officer would suffer. Moreover, such an officer would likely have a defense to any civil suit on the basis of qualified immunity.

Nor will it often be the case that any evidence that may be seized during the stop will be suppressed, thanks to the exception to the exclusionary rule for good-faith police errors. It is true that, unlike most States, North Carolina does not provide a good-faith exception as a matter of state law, but North Carolina recognizes that it may solve any remedial problems it may perceive on its own. More fundamentally, that is a remedial concern, and the protections offered by the Fourth Amendment are not meant to yield to accommodate remedial concerns. Our jurisprudence draws a sharp analytical distinction between the existence of a Fourth Amendment violation and the remedy for that violation.

In short, there is nothing in our case law requiring us to hold that a reasonable mistake of law can justify a seizure under the Fourth Amendment, and quite a bit suggesting just the opposite. I also see nothing to be gained from such a holding, and much to be lost. . . .

To my mind, the more administrable approach—and the one more consistent with our precedents and principles—would be to hold that an officer's mistake of law, no matter how reasonable, cannot support the individualized suspicion necessary to justify a seizure under the Fourth Amendment. I respectfully dissent.

Page 67. Add the following material at the end of note 1.

Compare State v. Peterson, 135 A.3d 686 (Conn. 2016) (drug suspect who carried "weighted" plastic bag provided police with reasonable suspicion, when combined with information about suspect's potential drug distribution over six months).

4. Criminal Profiles and Race

Page 86. Add the following material at the end of note 2.

As it becomes more common for local advocacy groups to analyze and publish data regarding traffic stops and pedestrian stops, police department leaders join in public debates about the meaning of the stop data. When reports show that the police stop drivers of a particular race at a disproportionate rate, police chiefs often point out the difficulty of knowing why officers make stops, and whether race is truly part of the officer's thinking. They sometimes point out that the use of census numbers to estimate the racial mix of a local population might not measure accurately the racial mix of drivers in a given location where patrols operate. That claim, in turn, raises the question of how the police choose particular locations for heavier enforcement efforts. See Joey Garrison, Nashville Police Chief Slams Racial Profiling Report as "Morally Disingenuous," The Tennessean, Mar. 7, 2017.

Page 96. Add the following material at the end of note 3.

In December 2014, the U.S. Department of Justice issued a guidance document placing limits on the use of race when federal agents develop reasonable suspicion to justify a stop. See https://www.justice.gov/sites/default/files/ag/pages/attachments/2014/12/08/use-of-race-policy.pdf. In August 2015, Maryland Attorney General Brian Frosh issued comparable guidance to state law enforcement agents. A state statute already generally barred racial profiling in the state; the policy specified that law enforcement officers may not consider personal characteristics while "conducting routine police activity." They may do so only if they have "credible information" that such characteristics are "directly relevant" to the investigation of a crime. The policy appears at www.marylandattorneygeneral.gov/Reports/Ending_Discriminatory_Profiling.pdf.

D. Brief Searches of Individuals

1. Frisks for Weapons

Page 128. Add the following material at the end of note 5.

During the fiftieth anniversary of the *Terry* decision, many scholars asked about the net impact of the decision on police practices and public, safety. See Jeffrey Fagan, Terry's Original Sin, 16 Univ. Chicago Legal Forum 43 (2016) (asking "whether the dilution and expansion of standards for an investigative stop over time compromised or advanced the very law enforcement interests that animated the *Terry* opinion").

2. The Scope of a *Terry* Search

Page 133. Add the following material before Problem 2-8.

Dennys Rodriguez v. United States

135 S. Ct. 1609 (2015)

GINSBURG, J.*

In Illinois v. Caballes, 543 U.S. 405 (2005), this Court held that a dog sniff conducted during a lawful traffic stop does not violate the Fourth Amendment's proscription of unreasonable seizures. This case presents the question whether the Fourth Amendment tolerates a dog sniff conducted after completion of a traffic stop. We hold that a police stop exceeding the time needed to handle the matter for which the stop was made violates the Constitution's shield against unreasonable seizures. A seizure justified only by a police-observed traffic violation, therefore, becomes unlawful "if it is prolonged beyond the time reasonably required to complete the mission" of issuing a ticket for the violation. The Court so recognized in *Caballes,* and we adhere to the line drawn in that decision.

Just after midnight on March 27, 2012, police officer Morgan Struble observed a Mercury Mountaineer veer slowly onto the shoulder of Nebraska State Highway 275 for one or two seconds and then jerk back onto the road. Nebraska law prohibits driving on highway shoulders, and on that basis, Struble pulled the Mountaineer over at 12:06 A.M. Struble is a K–9 officer with the Valley Police Department in Nebraska, and his dog Floyd was in his patrol car that night. Two men were in the Mountaineer: the driver, Dennys Rodriguez, and a front-seat passenger, Scott Pollman.

Struble approached the Mountaineer on the passenger's side. After Rodriguez identified himself, Struble asked him why he had driven onto the shoulder. Rodriguez replied that he had swerved to avoid a pothole. Struble then gathered Rodriguez's license, registration, and proof of insurance, and asked Rodriguez to accompany him to the patrol car. Rodriguez asked if he was required to do so, and Struble answered that he was not. Rodriguez decided to wait in his own vehicle.

[*Chief Justice Roberts and Justices Scalia, Breyer, Sotomayor, and Kagan joined this opinion—EDS.]

After running a records check on Rodriguez, Struble returned to the Mountaineer. Struble asked passenger Pollman for his driver's license and began to question him about where the two men were coming from and where they were going. Pollman replied that they had traveled to Omaha, Nebraska, to look at a Ford Mustang that was for sale and that they were returning to Norfolk, Nebraska. Struble returned again to his patrol car, where he completed a records check on Pollman, and called for a second officer. Struble then began writing a warning ticket for Rodriguez for driving on the shoulder of the road.

Struble returned to Rodriguez's vehicle a third time to issue the written warning. By 12:27 or 12:28 A.M., Struble had finished explaining the warning to Rodriguez, and had given back to Rodriguez and Pollman the documents obtained from them. As Struble later testified, at that point, Rodriguez and Pollman "had all their documents back and a copy of the written warning. I got all the reasons for the stop out of the way, . . . took care of all the business."

Nevertheless, Struble did not consider Rodriguez "free to leave." Although justification for the traffic stop was "out of the way," Struble asked for permission to walk his dog around Rodriguez's vehicle. Rodriguez said no. Struble then instructed Rodriguez to turn off the ignition, exit the vehicle, and stand in front of the patrol car to wait for the second officer. Rodriguez complied. At 12:33 A.M., a deputy sheriff arrived. Struble retrieved his dog and led him twice around the Mountaineer. The dog alerted to the presence of drugs halfway through Struble's second pass. All told, seven or eight minutes had elapsed from the time Struble issued the written warning until the dog indicated the presence of drugs. A search of the vehicle revealed a large bag of methamphetamine.

Rodriguez was indicted in the United States District Court for the District of Nebraska on one count of possession with intent to distribute 50 grams or more of methamphetamine. He moved to suppress the evidence seized from his car on the ground, among others, that Struble had prolonged the traffic stop without reasonable suspicion in order to conduct the dog sniff.

After receiving evidence, a Magistrate Judge recommended that the motion be denied. The Magistrate Judge found no probable cause to search the vehicle independent of the dog alert. He further found that no reasonable suspicion supported the detention once Struble issued the written warning. He concluded, however, that under Eighth Circuit precedent, extension of the stop by "seven to eight minutes" for the dog sniff was only a *de minimis* intrusion on Rodriguez's Fourth Amendment rights and was therefore permissible. . . . Rodriguez entered a conditional guilty plea and was sentenced to five years in prison. The Eighth Circuit affirmed. . . .

We granted certiorari to resolve a division among lower courts on the question whether police routinely may extend an otherwise-completed traffic stop, absent reasonable suspicion, in order to conduct a dog sniff.

A seizure for a traffic violation justifies a police investigation of that violation. A relatively brief encounter, a routine traffic stop is more analogous to a so-called "*Terry* stop" . . . than to a formal arrest. Like a *Terry* stop, the tolerable duration of police inquiries in the traffic-stop context is determined by the seizure's "mission" — to address the traffic violation that warranted the stop, and attend to related safety concerns. Because addressing the infraction is the purpose of the stop, it may last no longer than is necessary to effectuate that purpose. Authority for the seizure thus ends when tasks tied to the traffic infraction are — or reasonably should have been — completed.

Our decisions in *Caballes* and Arizona v. Johnson, 555 U.S. 323 (2009), heed these constraints. In both cases, we concluded that the Fourth Amendment tolerated certain unrelated investigations that did not lengthen the roadside detention. In *Caballes,* however, we cautioned that a traffic stop "can become unlawful if it is prolonged beyond the time reasonably required" to complete the mission of issuing a warning ticket. And we repeated that admonition in *Johnson*: The seizure remains lawful only so long as unrelated inquiries "do not measurably extend the duration of the stop." An officer, in other words, may conduct certain unrelated checks during an otherwise lawful traffic stop. But . . . he may not do so in a way that prolongs the stop, absent the reasonable suspicion ordinarily demanded to justify detaining an individual.

Beyond determining whether to issue a traffic ticket, an officer's mission includes "ordinary inquiries incident to [the traffic] stop." Typically such inquiries involve checking the driver's license, determining whether there are outstanding warrants against the driver, and inspecting the automobile's registration and proof of insurance. These checks serve the same objective as enforcement of the traffic code: ensuring that vehicles on the road are operated safely and responsibly.

A dog sniff, by contrast, is a measure aimed at detecting evidence of ordinary criminal wrongdoing. Candidly, the Government acknowledged at oral argument that a dog sniff, unlike the routine measures just mentioned, is not an ordinary incident of a traffic stop. Lacking the same close connection to roadway safety as the ordinary inquiries, a dog sniff is not fairly characterized as part of the officer's traffic mission.

In advancing its *de minimis* rule, the Eighth Circuit relied heavily on our decision in Pennsylvania v. Mimms, 434 U.S. 106 (1977) (per curiam). In *Mimms,* we reasoned that the government's "legitimate and weighty" interest in officer safety outweighs the "*de minimis*" additional intrusion of requiring a driver, already lawfully stopped, to exit the vehicle. . . .

Unlike a general interest in criminal enforcement, however, the government's officer safety interest stems from the mission of the stop itself. Traffic stops are especially fraught with danger to police officers, so an officer may need to take certain negligibly burdensome precautions in order to complete his mission safely. On-scene investigation into other crimes, however, detours from that mission. So too do safety precautions taken in order to facilitate such detours. Thus, even assuming that the imposition here was no more intrusive than the exit order in *Mimms,* the dog sniff could not be justified on the same basis. Highway and officer safety are interests different in kind from the Government's endeavor to detect crime in general or drug trafficking in particular.

The Government argues that an officer may "incrementally" prolong a stop to conduct a dog sniff so long as the officer is reasonably diligent in pursuing the traffic-related purpose of the stop, and the overall duration of the stop remains reasonable in relation to the duration of other traffic stops involving similar circumstances. The Government's argument, in effect, is that by completing all traffic-related tasks expeditiously, an officer can earn bonus time to pursue an unrelated criminal investigation. The reasonableness of a seizure, however, depends on what the police in fact do. In this regard, the Government acknowledges that "an officer always has to be reasonably diligent." How could diligence be gauged other than by noting what the officer actually did and how he did it? If an officer can complete traffic-based inquiries expeditiously, then that is the amount of "time reasonably required" to complete the stop's mission." As we said in *Caballes* and reiterate today, a traffic stop prolonged beyond that point is unlawful.

The critical question, then, is not whether the dog sniff occurs before or after the officer issues a ticket, but whether conducting the sniff "prolongs"—*i.e.,* adds time to—"the stop."

The Magistrate Judge found that detention for the dog sniff in this case was not independently supported by individualized suspicion, and the District Court adopted the Magistrate Judge's findings. The Court of Appeals, however, did not review that determination. The question whether reasonable suspicion of criminal activity justified detaining Rodriguez beyond completion of the traffic infraction investigation, therefore, remains open for Eighth Circuit consideration on remand. . . .

THOMAS, J., dissenting.[*]

Ten years ago, we explained that "conducting a dog sniff [does] not change the character of a traffic stop that is lawful at its inception and otherwise executed in a reasonable manner." Illinois v. Caballes, 543 U.S. 405 (2005). The only question here is whether an officer executed a stop in a reasonable manner when he waited to conduct a dog sniff until after he had given the driver a written warning and a backup unit had arrived, bringing the overall duration of the stop to 29 minutes. Because the stop was reasonably executed, no Fourth Amendment violation occurred. . . .

Because Rodriguez does not dispute that Officer Struble had probable cause to stop him, the only question is whether the stop was otherwise executed in a reasonable manner. I easily conclude that it was. Approximately 29 minutes passed from the time Officer Struble stopped Rodriguez until his narcotics-detection dog alerted to the presence of drugs. That amount of time is hardly out of the ordinary for a traffic stop by a single officer of a vehicle containing multiple occupants even when no dog sniff is involved. During that time, Officer Struble conducted the ordinary activities of a traffic stop — he approached the vehicle, questioned Rodriguez about the observed violation, asked Pollman about their travel plans, ran serial warrant checks on Rodriguez and Pollman, and issued a written warning to Rodriguez. And when he decided to conduct a dog sniff, he took the precaution of calling for backup out of concern for his safety. . . .

The majority's rule requires a traffic stop to end when "tasks tied to the traffic infraction are—or reasonably should have been—completed."

[[*]Justice Alito joined this opinion; Justice Kennedy joined except as to Part III—EDS.]

. . . The majority's rule thus imposes a one-way ratchet for constitutional protection linked to the characteristics of the individual officer conducting the stop: If a driver is stopped by a particularly efficient officer, then he will be entitled to be released from the traffic stop after a shorter period of time than a driver stopped by a less efficient officer. Similarly, if a driver is stopped by an officer with access to technology that can shorten a records check, then he will be entitled to be released from the stop after a shorter period of time than an individual stopped by an officer without access to such technology. I cannot accept that the search and seizure protections of the Fourth Amendment are so variable and can be made to turn upon such trivialities. . . .

The majority's logic would produce similarly arbitrary results. Under its reasoning, a traffic stop made by a rookie could be executed in a reasonable manner, whereas the same traffic stop made by a knowledgeable, veteran officer *in precisely the same circumstances* might not, if in fact his knowledge and experience made him capable of completing the stop faster. We have long rejected interpretations of the Fourth Amendment that would produce such haphazard results, and I see no reason to depart from our consistent practice today.

As if that were not enough, the majority also limits the duration of the stop to the time it takes the officer to complete a narrow category of "traffic-based inquiries." According to the majority, these inquiries include those that "serve the same objective as enforcement of the traffic code: ensuring that vehicles on the road are operated safely and responsibly." Inquiries directed to "detecting evidence of ordinary criminal wrongdoing" are not traffic-related inquiries and thus cannot count toward the overall duration of the stop. . . .

The majority's approach draws an artificial line between dog sniffs and other common police practices. The lower courts have routinely confirmed that warrant checks are a constitutionally permissible part of a traffic stop, and the majority confirms that it finds no fault in these measures. Yet its reasoning suggests the opposite. . . .

Investigative questioning rests on the same basis as the dog sniff. . . . The majority's reasoning appears to allow officers to engage in *some* questioning aimed at detecting evidence of ordinary criminal wrongdoing. But it is hard to see how such inquiries fall within the seizure's "mission" of addressing the traffic violation that warranted the stop, or attending to "related safety concerns." Its reasoning appears to come down to the principle that dogs are different. . . .

Had Officer Struble arrested, handcuffed, and taken Rodriguez to the police station for his traffic violation, he would have complied with the Fourth Amendment. But because he made Rodriguez wait for seven or eight extra minutes until a dog arrived, he evidently committed a constitutional violation. Such a view of the Fourth Amendment makes little sense. . . .

Today's revision of our Fourth Amendment jurisprudence was also entirely unnecessary. Rodriguez suffered no Fourth Amendment violation here for an entirely independent reason: Officer Struble had reasonable suspicion to continue to hold him for investigative purposes. . . .

Officer Struble testified that he first became suspicious that Rodriguez was engaged in criminal activity for a number of reasons. When he approached the vehicle, he smelled an "overwhelming odor of air freshener coming from the vehicle," which is, in his experience, "a common attempt to conceal an odor that [people] don't want . . . to be smelled by the police." He also observed, upon approaching the front window on the passenger side of the vehicle, that Rodriguez's passenger, Scott Pollman, appeared nervous. Pollman pulled his hat down low, puffed nervously on a cigarette, and refused to make eye contact with him. The officer thought he was "more nervous than your typical passenger" who "doesn't have anything to worry about" because they didn't commit a traffic violation.

Officer Struble's interactions with the vehicle's occupants only increased his suspicions. When he asked Rodriguez why he had driven onto the shoulder, Rodriguez claimed that he swerved to avoid a pothole. But that story could not be squared with Officer Struble's observation of the vehicle slowly driving off the road before being jerked back onto it. And when Officer Struble asked Pollman where they were coming from and where they were going, Pollman told him they were traveling from Omaha, Nebraska, back to Norfolk, Nebraska, after looking at a vehicle they were considering purchasing. Pollman told the officer that he had neither seen pictures of the vehicle nor confirmed title before the trip. As Officer Struble explained, it "seemed suspicious" to him to drive "approximately two hours . . . late at night to see a vehicle sight unseen to possibly buy it," and to go from Norfolk to Omaha to look at it because "usually people leave Omaha to go get vehicles, not the other way around" due to higher Omaha taxes.

These facts, taken together, easily meet our standard for reasonable suspicion. Nervous, evasive behavior is a pertinent factor in determining reasonable suspicion, and both vehicle occupants were engaged in such conduct. The officer also recognized heavy use of air freshener, which, in his experience, indicated the presence of contraband in the vehicle. Commonsense judgments and inferences about human behavior further support the officer's conclusion that Pollman's story about their trip was likely a cover story for illegal activity. Taking into account all the relevant facts, Officer Struble possessed reasonable suspicion of criminal activity to conduct the dog sniff. . . .

ALITO, J., dissenting.

This is an unnecessary, impractical, and arbitrary decision. It addresses a purely hypothetical question: whether the traffic stop in this case *would be* unreasonable if the police officer, prior to leading a drug-sniffing dog around the exterior of petitioner's car, did not already have reasonable suspicion that the car contained drugs. In fact, however, the police officer *did have* reasonable suspicion, and, as a result, the officer was justified in detaining the occupants for the short period of time (seven or eight minutes) that is at issue. . . .

The Court refuses to address the real Fourth Amendment question: whether the stop was unreasonably prolonged. Instead, the Court latches onto the fact that Officer Struble delivered the warning prior to the dog sniff and proclaims that the authority to detain based on a traffic stop ends when a citation or warning is handed over to the driver. The Court thus holds that the Fourth Amendment was violated, not because of the length of the stop, but simply because of the sequence in which Officer Struble chose to perform his tasks.

This holding is not only arbitrary; it is perverse since Officer Struble chose that sequence for the purpose of protecting his own safety and possibly the safety of others. Without prolonging the stop, Officer Struble could have conducted the dog sniff while one of the tasks that the Court regards as properly part of the traffic stop was still in progress, but that sequence would have entailed unnecessary risk. At approximately 12:19 A.M., after collecting Pollman's driver's license, Officer Struble did two things. He called in the information needed to do a records check on Pollman (a step that the Court recognizes was properly part of the traffic stop), and he requested that another officer report to the scene.

Officer Struble had decided to perform a dog sniff but did not want to do that without another officer present. When occupants of a vehicle who know that their vehicle contains a large amount of illegal drugs see that a drug-sniffing dog has alerted for the presence of drugs, they will almost certainly realize that the police will then proceed to search the vehicle, discover the drugs, and make arrests. Thus, it is reasonable for an officer to believe that an alert will increase the risk that the occupants of the vehicle will attempt to flee or perhaps even attack the officer.

In this case, Officer Struble was concerned that he was outnumbered at the scene, and he therefore called for backup and waited for the arrival of another officer before conducting the sniff. As a result, the sniff was not completed until seven or eight minutes after he delivered the warning. But Officer Struble could have proceeded with the dog sniff while he was waiting for the results of the records check on Pollman and before the arrival of the second officer. The drug-sniffing dog was present in Officer Struble's car. If he had chosen that riskier sequence of events, the dog sniff would have been completed before the point in time when, according to the Court's analysis, the authority to detain for the traffic stop ended. Thus, an action that would have been lawful had the officer made the *unreasonable* decision to risk his life became unlawful when the officer made the *reasonable* decision to wait a few minutes for backup. Officer Struble's error—apparently—was following prudent procedures motivated by legitimate safety concerns. The Court's holding therefore makes no practical sense. And nothing in the Fourth Amendment, which speaks of *reasonableness,* compels this arbitrary line.

The rule that the Court adopts will do little good going forward. It is unlikely to have any appreciable effect on the length of future traffic stops. Most officers will learn the prescribed sequence of events even if they cannot fathom the reason for that requirement. (I would love to be the proverbial fly on the wall when police instructors teach this rule to officers who make traffic stops.)

Chapter 3

Full Searches of People and Places: Basic Concepts

B. *Probable Cause*

1. Defining Probable Cause

Page 155. Insert the following material at the end of note 3.

In District of Columbia v. Wesby, 138 S. Ct. 577 (2018), officers arrested 21 attendees at a party in an unoccupied house for unlawful entry. They later filed a civil damages suit, challenging the officers' basis for probable cause to support their arrests; the Supreme Court held that the lower court erred in granting summary judgment, in part because the officers had sufficient facts to establish probable cause that the arrestees knew they entered the house without the owner's consent. Although the arrestees on the scene claimed that a lessee of the home gave them permission to conduct a party there, the Court pointed to other evidence supporting the charges: the near-abandoned nature of the house, the loud and unrestrained quality of the party activities, and the behavior of partygoers who fled when the police arrived and gave inconsistent answers to questions about the ownership of the house. These circumstances allowed the officers to make several "common-sense conclusions about human behavior." The Supreme Court also criticized the trial judge and the D.C. Circuit for engaging in an "excessively technical dissection" of the factors supporting probable cause by viewing each fact "in isolation, rather than as a factor in the totality of the circumstances," and by dismissing outright "any circumstances that were susceptible of innocent explanation."

C. Warrants

2. Requirements for Obtaining Warrants

Page 189. Insert the following material at the end of note 1.

Wheeler v. State, 135 A.3d 282 (Del. 2016) (search warrants in a witness tampering case that were "cut-and-pasted" from a child pornography warrant gave police too much leeway to rummage through the target's digital records and did not satisfy particularity requirement).

4. So You Like Warrants?

Page 207. Replace *Camara* with the following material.

City of Los Angeles v. Naranjibhai Patel
135 S. Ct. 2443 (2015)

SOTOMAYOR, J.[*]

Respondents brought a Fourth Amendment challenge to a provision of the Los Angeles Municipal Code that compels "every operator of a hotel to keep a record" containing specified information concerning guests and to make this record "available to any officer of the Los Angeles Police Department for inspection" on demand. Los Angeles Municipal Code

[* Justices Kennedy, Ginsburg, Breyer, and Kagan joined this opinion. Justices Scalia and Alito filed dissenting opinions—EDS.]

§§ 41.49(2), (3)(a), (4) (2015). The questions presented are whether facial challenges to statutes can be brought under the Fourth Amendment and, if so, whether this provision of the Los Angeles Municipal Code is facially invalid. We hold facial challenges can be brought under the Fourth Amendment. We further hold that the provision of the Los Angeles Municipal Code that requires hotel operators to make their registries available to the police on demand is facially unconstitutional because it penalizes them for declining to turn over their records without affording them any opportunity for precompliance review.

I.

Los Angeles Municipal Code (LAMC) § 41.49 requires hotel operators to record information about their guests, including: the guest's name and address; the number of people in each guest's party; the make, model, and license plate number of any guest's vehicle parked on hotel property; the guest's date and time of arrival and scheduled departure date; the room number assigned to the guest; the rate charged and amount collected for the room; and the method of payment. Guests without reservations, those who pay for their rooms with cash, and any guests who rent a room for less than 12 hours must present photographic identification at the time of check-in, and hotel operators are required to record the number and expiration date of that document. For those guests who check in using an electronic kiosk, the hotel's records must also contain the guest's credit card information. This information can be maintained in either electronic or paper form, but it must be "kept on the hotel premises in the guest reception or guest check-in area or in an office adjacent" thereto for a period of 90 days.

Section 41.49(3)(a)—the only provision at issue here—states, in pertinent part, that hotel guest records "shall be made available to any officer of the Los Angeles Police Department for inspection," provided that "whenever possible, the inspection shall be conducted at a time and in a manner that minimizes any interference with the operation of the business." A hotel operator's failure to make his or her guest records available for police inspection is a misdemeanor punishable by up to six months in jail and a $1,000 fine.

In 2003, respondents, a group of motel operators along with a lodging association, sued the city of Los Angeles in three consolidated cases challenging the constitutionality of § 41.49(3)(a). They sought declaratory and injunctive relief. The parties . . . stipulated that respondents have been subjected to mandatory record inspections under the ordinance without consent or a warrant.

Following a bench trial, the District Court entered judgment in favor of the City, holding that respondents' facial challenge failed because they lacked a reasonable expectation of privacy in the records subject to inspection. A divided panel of the Ninth Circuit affirmed on the same grounds. On rehearing en banc, however, the Court of Appeals reversed.

The en banc court first determined that a police officer's nonconsensual inspection of hotel records under § 41.49 is a Fourth Amendment "search" because the business records covered by § 41.49 are "the hotel's private property" and the hotel therefore "has the right to exclude others from prying" into their contents. Next, the court assessed "whether the searches authorized by § 41.49 are reasonable." Relying on Donovan v. Lone Steer, Inc., 464 U.S. 408 (1984), and See v. Seattle, 387 U.S. 541 (1967), the court held that § 41.49 is facially unconstitutional "as it authorizes inspections" of hotel records "without affording an opportunity to obtain judicial review of the reasonableness of the demand prior to suffering penalties for refusing to comply." . . .

II.

We first clarify that facial challenges under the Fourth Amendment are not categorically barred or especially disfavored. A facial challenge is an attack on a statute itself as opposed to a particular application. While such challenges are the most difficult to mount successfully, the Court has never held that these claims cannot be brought under any otherwise enforceable provision of the Constitution. Instead, the Court has allowed such challenges to proceed under a diverse array of constitutional provisions.

Fourth Amendment challenges to statutes authorizing warrantless searches are no exception. Any claim to the contrary reflects a misunderstanding of our decision in Sibron v. New York, 392 U.S. 40 (1968). [That case] stands for the simple proposition that claims for facial relief under the Fourth Amendment are unlikely to succeed when there is substantial ambiguity as to what conduct a statute authorizes: Where a statute consists of "extraordinarily elastic categories," it may be "impossible to tell" whether and to what extent it deviates from the requirements of the Fourth Amendment.

This reading of *Sibron* is confirmed by subsequent precedents.

Since *Sibron,* the Court has entertained facial challenges under the Fourth Amendment to statutes authorizing warrantless searches. Perhaps more importantly, the Court has on numerous occasions declared statutes facially invalid under the Fourth Amendment.

[When] addressing a facial challenge to a statute authorizing warrantless searches, the proper focus of the constitutional inquiry is searches that the law actually authorizes, not those for which it is irrelevant. If exigency or a warrant justifies an officer's search, the subject of the search must permit it to proceed irrespective of whether it is authorized by statute. . .

III.

Turning to the merits of the particular claim before us, we hold that § 41.49(3)(a) is facially unconstitutional because it fails to provide hotel operators with an opportunity for precompliance review.

A.

The Fourth Amendment protects "the right of the people to be secure in their persons, houses, papers, and effects, against unreasonable searches and seizures." It further provides that "no Warrants shall issue, but upon probable cause." Based on this constitutional text, the Court has repeatedly held that searches conducted outside the judicial process, without prior approval by a judge or a magistrate judge, are *per se* unreasonable . . . subject only to a few specifically established and well-delineated exceptions. This rule applies to commercial premises as well as to homes.

Search regimes where no warrant is ever required may be reasonable where "special needs . . . make the warrant and probable-cause requirement impracticable," and where the "primary purpose" of the searches is "distinguishable from the general interest in crime control." Here, we assume that the searches authorized by § 41.49 serve a "special need" other than conducting criminal investigations: They ensure compliance with the recordkeeping requirement, which in turn deters criminals from operating on the hotels' premises. The Court has referred to this kind of search as an "administrative search." Camara v. Municipal Court of City and County of San Francisco, 387 U.S. 523 (1967). Thus, we consider whether § 41.49 falls within the administrative search exception to the warrant requirement.

The Court has held that absent consent, exigent circumstances, or the like, in order for an administrative search to be constitutional, the subject of the search must be afforded an opportunity to obtain precompliance review before a neutral decisionmaker. And, we see no reason why this minimal requirement is inapplicable here. While the Court has never attempted to prescribe the exact form an opportunity for precompliance review must take, the City does not even attempt to argue that
§ 41.49(3)(a) affords hotel operators any opportunity whatsoever. Section 41.49(3)(a) is, therefore, facially invalid.

A hotel owner who refuses to give an officer access to his or her registry can be arrested on the spot. The Court has held that business owners cannot reasonably be put to this kind of choice. Absent an opportunity for precompliance review, the ordinance creates an intolerable risk that searches authorized by it will exceed statutory limits, or be used as a pretext to harass hotel operators and their guests. Even if a hotel has been searched 10 times a day, every day, for three months, without any violation being found, the operator can only refuse to comply with an officer's demand to turn over the registry at his or her own peril.

To be clear, we hold only that a hotel owner must be afforded an *opportunity* to have a neutral decisionmaker review an officer's demand to search the registry before he or she faces penalties for failing to comply. Actual review need only occur in those rare instances where a hotel operator objects to turning over the registry. Moreover, this opportunity can be provided without imposing onerous burdens on those charged with an administrative scheme's enforcement. For instance, respondents accept that the searches authorized by § 41.49(3)(a) would be constitutional if they were performed pursuant to an administrative subpoena. These subpoenas, which are typically a simple form, can be issued by the individual seeking the record—here, officers in the field—without probable cause that a regulation is being infringed. Issuing a subpoena will usually be the full extent of an officer's burden because "the great majority of businessmen can be expected in normal course to consent to inspection without warrant." Indeed, the City has cited no evidence suggesting that without an ordinance authorizing on-demand searches, hotel operators would regularly refuse to cooperate with the police.

In those instances, however, where a subpoenaed hotel operator believes that an attempted search is motivated by illicit purposes, respondents suggest it would be sufficient if he or she could move to quash the subpoena before any search takes place. A neutral decisionmaker, including an administrative law judge, would then review the subpoenaed party's objections before deciding whether the subpoena is enforceable. Given the limited grounds on which a motion to quash can be granted, such challenges will likely be rare. And, in the even rarer event that an officer reasonably suspects that a hotel operator may tamper with the registry while the motion to quash is pending, he or she can guard the registry until the required hearing can occur, which ought not take long. Riley v. California, 573 U.S. __ (2014) (police may seize and hold a cell phone "to prevent destruction of evidence while seeking a warrant"); Illinois v. McArthur, 531 U.S. 326 (2001) (citing cases upholding the constitutionality of "temporary restraints" where they are needed to preserve evidence until police could obtain a warrant). Cf. Missouri v. McNeely, 569 U.S. __ (2013) (noting that many States have procedures in place for considering warrant applications telephonically).

Procedures along these lines are ubiquitous. A 2002 report by the Department of Justice "identified approximately 335 existing administrative subpoena authorities held by various [federal] executive branch entities." Office of Legal Policy, Report to Congress on the Use of Administrative Subpoena Authorities by Executive Branch Agencies and Entities 3, online at http://www.justice.gov/archive/olp/rpt_to_congress.htm (All Internet materials as visited June 19, 2015, and available in Clerk of Court's case file). Their prevalence confirms what common sense alone would otherwise lead us to conclude: In most contexts, business owners can be afforded at least an opportunity to contest an administrative search's propriety without unduly compromising the government's ability to achieve its regulatory aims.

Of course administrative subpoenas are only one way in which an opportunity for precompliance review can be made available. But whatever the precise form, the availability of precompliance review alters the dynamic between the officer and the hotel to be searched, and reduces the risk that officers will use these administrative searches as a pretext to harass business owners.

Finally, we underscore the narrow nature of our holding. Respondents have not challenged and nothing in our opinion calls into question those parts of § 41.49 that require hotel operators to maintain guest registries containing certain information. And, even absent legislative action to create a procedure along the lines discussed above, police will not be prevented from obtaining access to these documents. As they often do, hotel operators remain free to consent to searches of their registries and police can compel them to turn them over if they have a proper administrative warrant—including one that was issued *ex parte*—or if some other exception to the warrant requirement applies, including exigent circumstances.

B.

Rather than arguing that § 41.49(3)(a) is constitutional under the general administrative search doctrine, the City and Justice Scalia contend that hotels are "closely regulated," and that the ordinance is facially valid under the more relaxed standard that applies to searches of this category of businesses. They are wrong on both counts.

Over the past 45 years, the Court has identified only four industries that "have such a history of government oversight that no reasonable expectation of privacy . . . could exist for a proprietor over the stock of such an enterprise." Simply listing these industries refutes petitioner's argument that hotels should be counted among them. Unlike liquor sales, firearms dealing, mining, or running an automobile junkyard, nothing inherent in the operation of hotels poses a clear and significant risk to the public welfare.

Moreover, "the clear import of our cases is that the closely regulated industry . . . is the exception." To classify hotels as pervasively regulated would permit what has always been a narrow exception to swallow the rule. The City wisely refrains from arguing that § 41.49 itself renders hotels closely regulated. Nor do any of the other regulations on which petitioner and Justice Scalia rely—regulations requiring hotels to, *inter alia,* maintain a license, collect taxes, conspicuously post their rates, and meet certain sanitary standards—establish a comprehensive scheme of regulation that distinguishes hotels from numerous other businesses. . . . If such general regulations were sufficient to invoke the closely regulated industry exception, it would be hard to imagine a type of business that would not qualify.

Petitioner attempts to recast this hodgepodge of regulations as a comprehensive scheme by referring to a "centuries-old tradition" of warrantless searches of hotels. History is relevant when determining whether an industry is closely regulated. The historical record here, however, is not as clear as petitioner suggests. . . .

Even if we were to find that hotels are pervasively regulated, §41.49 would need to satisfy three additional criteria to be reasonable under the Fourth Amendment: (1) There must be a "substantial" government interest that informs the regulatory scheme pursuant to which the inspection is made; (2) the warrantless inspections must be "necessary" to further the regulatory scheme; and (3) the statute's inspection program, in terms of the certainty and regularity of its application, must provide a constitutionally adequate substitute for a warrant. We assume petitioner's interest in ensuring that hotels maintain accurate and complete registries might fulfill the first of these requirements, but conclude that § 41.49 fails the second and third prongs of this test.

The City claims that affording hotel operators any opportunity for precompliance review would fatally undermine the scheme's efficacy by giving operators a chance to falsify their records. The Court has previously rejected this exact argument, which could be made regarding any recordkeeping requirement. We see no reason to accept it here.

As explained above, nothing in our decision today precludes an officer from conducting a surprise inspection by obtaining an *ex parte* warrant or, where an officer reasonably suspects the registry would be altered, from guarding the registry pending a hearing on a motion to quash. Justice Scalia's claim that these procedures will prove unworkable given the large number of hotels in Los Angeles is a red herring. While there are approximately 2,000 hotels in Los Angeles, there is no basis to believe that resort to such measures will be needed to conduct spot checks in the vast majority of them.

Section 41.49 is also constitutionally deficient under the "certainty and regularity" prong of the closely regulated industries test because it fails sufficiently to constrain police officers' discretion as to which hotels to search and under what circumstances. While the Court has upheld inspection schemes of closely regulated industries that called for searches at least four times a year, or on a "regular basis," § 41.49 imposes no comparable standard.

For the foregoing reasons, we agree with the Ninth Circuit that § 41.49(3)(a) is facially invalid insofar as it fails to provide any opportunity for precompliance review before a hotel must give its guest registry to the police for inspection. Accordingly, the judgment of the Ninth Circuit is affirmed.

SCALIA, J., dissenting.*

The city of Los Angeles, like many jurisdictions across the country, has a law that requires motels, hotels, and other places of overnight accommodation (hereinafter motels) to keep a register containing specified information about their guests. The purpose of this recordkeeping requirement is to deter criminal conduct, on the theory that criminals will be unwilling to carry on illicit activities in motel rooms if they must provide identifying information at check-in. Because this deterrent effect will only be accomplished if motels actually do require guests to provide the required information, the ordinance also authorizes police to conduct random spot checks of motels' guest registers to ensure that they are properly maintained. The ordinance limits these spot checks to the four corners of the register, and does not authorize police to enter any nonpublic area of the motel. To the extent possible, police must conduct these spot checks at times that will minimize any disruption to a motel's business.

The parties do not dispute the governmental interests at stake. Motels not only provide housing to vulnerable transient populations, they are also a particularly attractive site for criminal activity ranging from drug dealing and prostitution to human trafficking. Offering privacy and anonymity on the cheap, they have been employed as prisons for migrants smuggled across the border and held for ransom, and rendezvous sites where child sex workers meet their clients on threat of violence from their procurers.

Nevertheless, the Court today concludes that Los Angeles's ordinance is "unreasonable" inasmuch as it permits police to flip through a guest register to ensure it is being filled out without first providing an opportunity for the motel operator to seek judicial review. Because I believe that such a limited inspection of a guest register is eminently reasonable under the circumstances presented, I dissent. . . .

One exception to normal warrant requirements applies to searches of closely regulated businesses. When an entrepreneur embarks upon such a business, he has voluntarily chosen to subject himself to a "full arsenal of governmental regulation," and so a warrantless search to enforce those regulations is not unreasonable. Recognizing that warrantless searches of closely regulated businesses may nevertheless

* [Chief Justice Roberts and Justice Thomas joined this opinion—EDS.]

become unreasonable if arbitrarily conducted, we have required laws authorizing such searches to satisfy three criteria: (1) There must be a "substantial" government interest that informs the regulatory scheme pursuant to which the inspection is made; (2) the warrantless inspections must be "necessary" to further the regulatory scheme; and (3) the statute's inspection program, in terms of the certainty and regularity of its application, must provide a constitutionally adequate substitute for a warrant. Los Angeles's ordinance easily meets these standards.

In determining whether a business is closely regulated, this Court has looked to factors including the duration of the regulatory tradition, the comprehensiveness of the regulatory regime, and the imposition of similar regulations by other jurisdictions. These factors are not talismans, but shed light on the expectation of privacy the owner of a business may reasonably have, which in turn affects the reasonableness of a warrantless search.

Reflecting the unique public role of motels and their commercial forebears, governments have long subjected these businesses to unique public duties, and have established inspection regimes to ensure compliance. . . . And the tradition continues in Los Angeles.

The regulatory regime at issue here is . . . substantially *more* comprehensive than the regulations governing junkyards in *Burger,* where licensing, inventory-recording, and permit-posting requirements were found sufficient to qualify the industry as closely regulated. . . .

Finally, this ordinance is not an outlier. The City has pointed us to more than 100 similar register-inspection laws in cities and counties across the country, and that is far from exhaustive. In all, municipalities in at least 41 States have laws similar to Los Angeles's, and at least 8 States have their own laws authorizing register inspections.

This copious evidence is surely enough to establish that when a motel operator "chooses to engage in this pervasively regulated business . . . he does so with the knowledge that his business records . . . will be subject to effective inspection." And *that* is the relevant constitutional test. . . .

The City's ordinance easily satisfies the remaining *Burger* requirements: It furthers a substantial governmental interest, it is necessary to achieving that interest, and it provides an adequate substitute for a search warrant. Neither respondents nor the Court question the substantial interest of the City in deterring criminal activity.

The private pain and public costs imposed by drug dealing, prostitution, and human trafficking are beyond contention, and motels provide an obvious haven for those who trade in human misery. Warrantless inspections are also necessary to advance this interest. Although the Court acknowledges that law enforcement can enter a motel room without a warrant when exigent circumstances exist, the whole reason criminals use motel rooms in the first place is that they offer privacy and secrecy, so that police will never come to discover these exigencies. . . .

An administrative, warrantless-search ordinance that narrowly limits the scope of searches to a single business record, that does not authorize entry upon premises not open to the public, and that is supported by the need to prevent fabrication of guest registers, is, to say the least, far afield from the laws at issue in the cases the Court relies upon. The Court concludes that such minor intrusions, permissible when the police are trying to tamp down the market in stolen auto parts, are "unreasonable" when police are instead attempting to stamp out the market in child sex slaves.

Because I believe that the limited warrantless searches authorized by Los Angeles's ordinance are reasonable under the circumstances, I respectfully dissent.

Chapter 4

Searches in Recurring Contexts

A. *"Persons"*

1. Searches Incident to Arrest

Page 240. Insert this material at the end of note 1.

See also People v. Jenkins, 20 N.E.3d 639 (N.Y. 2014) (police who entered apartment after seeing armed man flee inside had no authority to search for the missing gun in a closed box after they handcuffed suspect and secured the premises).

2. Intrusive Body Searches

Page 250. Insert this material before the Notes.

Danny Birchfield v. North Dakota

576 U.S. ___ (2016)

ALITO, J.*

Drunk drivers take a grisly toll on the Nation's roads, claiming thousands of lives, injuring many more victims, and inflicting billions of dollars in property damage every year. To fight this problem, all States have laws that prohibit motorists from driving with a blood alcohol concentration (BAC) that exceeds a specified level. But determining whether a driver's BAC is over the legal limit requires a test, and many drivers stopped on suspicion of drunk driving would not submit to testing if given the option. So every State also has long had what are termed "implied consent laws." These laws impose penalties on motorists who refuse to undergo testing when there is sufficient reason to believe they are violating the State's drunk-driving laws.

In the past, the typical penalty for noncompliance was suspension or revocation of the motorist's license. The cases now before us involve laws that go beyond that and make it a crime for a motorist to refuse to be tested after being lawfully arrested for driving while impaired. The question presented is whether such laws violate the Fourth Amendment's prohibition against unreasonable searches. . . .

Enforcement of laws of this type obviously requires the measurement of BAC. One way of doing this is to analyze a sample of a driver's blood directly. A technician with medical training uses a syringe to draw a blood sample from the veins of the subject, who must remain still during the procedure, and then the sample is shipped to a separate laboratory for measurement of its alcohol concentration. Although it is possible for a subject to be forcibly immobilized so that a sample may be drawn, many States prohibit drawing blood from a driver who resists

* [Justices Kennedy, Ginsburg, Breyer, and Kagan joined this opinion. Justices Scalia and Alito filed dissenting opinions.—EDS.]

since this practice helps "to avoid violent confrontations." The most common and economical method of calculating BAC is by means of a machine [such as a "Breathalyzer"] that measures the amount of alcohol in a person's breath. . . . Measurement of BAC based on a breath test requires the cooperation of the person being tested. The subject must take a deep breath and exhale through a mouthpiece that connects to the machine. Typically the test subject must blow air into the device for a period of several seconds to produce an adequate breath sample, and the process is sometimes repeated so that analysts can compare multiple samples to ensure the device's accuracy. . . . When a standard infrared device is used, the whole process takes only a few minutes from start to finish. Most evidentiary breath tests do not occur next to the vehicle, at the side of the road, but in a police station, where the controlled environment is especially conducive to reliable testing, or in some cases in the officer's patrol vehicle or in special mobile testing facilities.

Because the cooperation of the test subject is necessary when a breath test is administered and highly preferable when a blood sample is taken, the enactment of laws defining intoxication based on BAC made it necessary for States to find a way of securing such cooperation. So-called "implied consent" laws were enacted to achieve this result. They provided that cooperation with BAC testing was a condition of the privilege of driving on state roads and that the privilege would be rescinded if a suspected drunk driver refused to honor that condition. . . . Suspension or revocation of the motorist's driver's license remains the standard legal consequence of refusal. In addition, evidence of the motorist's refusal is admitted as evidence of likely intoxication in a drunk-driving prosecution. . . .

If the penalty for driving with a greatly elevated BAC or for repeat violations exceeds the penalty for refusing to submit to testing, motorists who fear conviction for the more severely punished offenses have an incentive to reject testing. And in some States, the refusal rate is high. On average, over one-fifth of all drivers asked to submit to BAC testing in 2011 refused to do so. In North Dakota, the refusal rate for 2011 was a representative 21%.

To combat the problem of test refusal, some States have begun to enact laws making it a crime to refuse to undergo testing. North Dakota adopted [such a law] in 2013, after a pair of drunk-driving accidents claimed the lives of an entire young family and another family's 5- and 9-year-old boys. . . .

Petitioner Danny Birchfield accidentally drove his car off a North Dakota highway on October 10, 2013. A state trooper arrived and watched as Birchfield unsuccessfully tried to drive back out of the ditch in which his car was stuck. The trooper approached, caught a strong whiff of alcohol, and saw that Birchfield's eyes were bloodshot and watery. Birchfield spoke in slurred speech and struggled to stay steady on his feet. At the trooper's request, Birchfield agreed to take several field sobriety tests and performed poorly on each. He had trouble reciting sections of the alphabet and counting backwards in compliance with the trooper's directions.

Believing that Birchfield was intoxicated, the trooper informed him of his obligation under state law to agree to a BAC test. Birchfield consented to a roadside breath test. The device used for this sort of test often differs from the machines used for breath tests administered in a police station and is intended to provide a preliminary assessment of the driver's BAC. Because the reliability of these preliminary or screening breath tests varies, many jurisdictions do not permit their numerical results to be admitted in a drunk-driving trial as evidence of a driver's BAC. In North Dakota, results from this type of test are "used only for determining whether or not a further test shall be given." In Birchfield's case, the screening test estimated that his BAC was 0.254%, more than three times the legal limit of 0.08%.

The state trooper arrested Birchfield for driving while impaired, gave the usual *Miranda* warnings, again advised him of his obligation under North Dakota law to undergo BAC testing, and informed him, as state law requires, that refusing to take the test would expose him to criminal penalties. In addition to mandatory addiction treatment, sentences range from a mandatory fine of $500 (for first-time offenders) to fines of at least $2,000 and imprisonment of at least one year and one day (for serial offenders). These criminal penalties apply to blood, breath, and urine test refusals alike.

Although faced with the prospect of prosecution under this law, Birchfield refused to let his blood be drawn. Just three months before, Birchfield had received a citation for driving under the influence, and he ultimately pleaded guilty to that offense. This time he also pleaded guilty—to a misdemeanor violation of the refusal statute—but his plea was a conditional one: while Birchfield admitted refusing the blood test, he argued that the Fourth Amendment prohibited criminalizing his refusal to submit to the test. The State District Court rejected this argument and imposed a sentence that accounted for his prior conviction. The sentence included 30 days in jail (20 of which were suspended and 10 of which had already been served), 1 year of unsupervised probation, $1,750 in fine and fees, and mandatory participation in a sobriety program and in a substance abuse evaluation. On appeal, the North Dakota Supreme Court affirmed.

[The Court also described the facts and proceedings in two companion cases, involving petitioners Beylund and Bernard.] We granted certiorari in all three cases and consolidated them for argument in order to decide whether motorists lawfully arrested for drunk driving may be convicted of a crime or otherwise penalized for refusing to take a warrantless test measuring the alcohol in their bloodstream. [Success] for all three petitioners depends on the proposition that the criminal law ordinarily may not compel a motorist to submit to the taking of a blood sample or to a breath test unless a warrant authorizing such testing is issued by a magistrate. If, on the other hand, such warrantless searches comport with the Fourth Amendment, it follows that a State may criminalize the refusal to comply with a demand to submit to the required testing, just as a State may make it a crime for a person to obstruct the execution of a valid search warrant. And by the same token, if such warrantless searches are constitutional, there is no obstacle under federal law to the admission of the results that they yield in either a criminal prosecution or a civil or administrative proceeding. We therefore begin by considering whether the searches demanded in these cases were consistent with the Fourth Amendment. . . .

The Fourth Amendment . . . prohibits "unreasonable searches," and our cases establish that the taking of a blood sample or the administration of a breath test is a search. See Skinner v. Railway Labor Executives' Assn., 489 U.S. 602 (1989); Schmerber v. California, 384 U.S. 757 (1966). The question, then, is whether the warrantless searches at issue here were reasonable.

The text of the Fourth Amendment does not specify when a search warrant must be obtained. But this Court has inferred that a warrant must [usually] be secured. This usual requirement, however, is subject to a number of exceptions. We have previously had occasion to examine whether one such exception—for "exigent circumstances"—applies in drunk-driving investigations. The exigent circumstances exception allows a warrantless search when an emergency leaves police insufficient time to seek a warrant. It permits, for instance, the warrantless entry of private property when there is a need to provide urgent aid to those inside, when police are in hot pursuit of a fleeing suspect, and when police fear the imminent destruction of evidence.

In Schmerber v. California, we held that drunk driving *may* present such an exigency. There, an officer directed hospital personnel to take a blood sample from a driver who was receiving treatment for car crash injuries. The Court concluded that the officer "might reasonably have believed that he was confronted with an emergency" that left no time to seek a warrant because "the percentage of alcohol in the blood begins to diminish shortly after drinking stops." On the specific facts of that case, where time had already been lost taking the driver to the hospital and investigating the accident, the Court found no Fourth Amendment violation even though the warrantless blood draw took place over the driver's objection.

More recently, though, we have held that the natural dissipation of alcohol from the bloodstream does not *always* constitute an exigency justifying the warrantless taking of a blood sample. That was the holding of Missouri v. McNeely, 133 S. Ct. 1552 (2013), where the State of Missouri was seeking a *per se* rule that "whenever an officer has probable cause to believe an individual has been driving under the influence of alcohol, exigent circumstances will necessarily exist because BAC evidence is inherently evanescent." We disagreed, emphasizing that *Schmerber* had adopted a case-specific analysis depending on "all of the facts and circumstances of the particular case." . . . While emphasizing that the exigent-circumstances exception must be applied on a case-by-case basis, the *McNeely* Court noted that other exceptions to the warrant requirement "apply categorically" rather than in a "case-specific" fashion. One of these, as the *McNeely* opinion recognized, is the long-established rule that a warrantless search may be conducted incident to a lawful arrest. But the Court pointedly did not address any potential justification for warrantless testing of drunk-driving suspects except for the exception at issue in the case, namely, the exception for exigent circumstances. . . .

In the three cases now before us, the drivers were searched or told that they were required to submit to a search after being placed under arrest for drunk driving. We therefore consider how the search-incident-to-arrest doctrine applies to breath and blood tests incident to such arrests.

The search-incident-to-arrest doctrine has an ancient pedigree. Well before the Nation's founding, it was recognized that officers carrying out a lawful arrest had the authority to make a warrantless search of the arrestee's person. . . . One Fourth Amendment historian has observed that, prior to American independence, anyone arrested "could expect that not only his surface clothing but his body, luggage, and saddlebags would be searched and, perhaps, his shoes, socks, and mouth as well." W. Cuddihy, The Fourth Amendment: Origins and Original Meaning (2009). No historical evidence suggests that the Fourth Amendment altered the permissible bounds of arrestee searches. . . .

We attempted to clarify the law regarding searches incident to arrest in Chimel v. California, 395 U.S. 752, 754 (1969), a case in which officers had searched the arrestee's entire three-bedroom house. *Chimel* endorsed a general rule that arresting officers, in order to prevent the arrestee from obtaining a weapon or destroying evidence, could search both "the person arrested" and "the area within his immediate control." No comparable justification, we said, supported "routinely searching any room other than that in which an arrest occurs—or, for that matter, for searching through all the desk drawers or other closed or concealed areas in that room itself."

Four years later, in United States v. Robinson, 414 U.S. 218 (1973), we elaborated on *Chimel*'s meaning. We noted that the search-incident-to-arrest rule actually comprises two distinct propositions: "The first is that a search may be made of the *person* of the arrestee by virtue of the lawful arrest. The second is that a search may be made of the area within the control of the arrestee." After a thorough review of the relevant common law history, we repudiated "case-by-case adjudication" of the question whether an arresting officer had the authority to carry out a search of the arrestee's person. The permissibility of such searches, we held, does not depend on whether a search of a *particular* arrestee is likely to protect officer safety or evidence: "The authority to search the person incident to a lawful custodial arrest, while based upon the need to disarm and to discover evidence, does not depend on what a court may later decide was the probability in a particular arrest situation that weapons or evidence would in fact be found upon the person of the suspect." Instead, the mere "fact of the lawful arrest" justifies "a full search of the person." In *Robinson* itself, that meant that police had acted permissibly in searching inside a package of cigarettes found on the man they arrested.

Our decision two Terms ago in Riley v. California, 573 U.S. ___ (2014), reaffirmed *Robinson*'s categorical rule and explained how the rule should be applied in situations that could not have been envisioned when the Fourth Amendment was adopted. *Riley* concerned a search of data contained in the memory of a modern cell phone. "Absent more precise guidance from the founding era," the Court wrote, "we generally determine whether to exempt a given type of search from the warrant requirement by assessing, on the one hand, the degree to which it intrudes upon an individual's privacy and, on the other, the degree to which it is needed for the promotion of legitimate governmental interests."

Blood and breath tests to measure blood alcohol concentration are not as new as searches of cell phones, but here, as in *Riley*, the founding era does not provide any definitive guidance as to whether they should be allowed incident to arrest. Lacking such guidance, we engage in the same mode of analysis as in *Riley*: we examine the degree to which they intrude upon an individual's privacy and "the degree to which [they are] needed for the promotion of legitimate governmental interests."

We begin by considering the impact of breath and blood tests on individual privacy interests, and we will discuss each type of test in turn.

Years ago we said that breath tests do not implicate "significant privacy concerns." *Skinner*. That remains so today. First, the physical intrusion is almost negligible. Breath tests do not require piercing the skin and entail a minimum of inconvenience. [The] process requires the arrestee to blow continuously for 4 to 15 seconds into a straw-like mouthpiece that is connected by a tube to the test machine. . . . The effort is no more demanding than blowing up a party balloon.

Petitioner Bernard argues, however, that the process is nevertheless a significant intrusion because the arrestee must insert the mouthpiece of the machine into his or her mouth. But there is nothing painful or strange about this requirement. The use of a straw to drink beverages is a common practice and one to which few object. . . .

Nor, contrary to Bernard, is the test a significant intrusion because it "does not capture an ordinary exhalation of the kind that routinely is exposed to the public" but instead requires a sample of "alveolar" (deep lung) air. Humans have never been known to assert a possessory interest in or any emotional attachment to *any* of the air in their lungs. The air that humans exhale is not part of their bodies. Exhalation is a natural process—indeed, one that is necessary for life. Humans cannot hold their breath for more than a few minutes, and all the air that is breathed into a breath analyzing machine, including deep lung air, sooner or later would be exhaled even without the test.

In prior cases, we have upheld warrantless searches involving physical intrusions that were at least as significant as that entailed in the administration of a breath test. Just recently we described the process of collecting a DNA sample by rubbing a swab on the inside of a person's cheek as a "negligible" intrusion. Maryland v. King, 569 U.S. ___ (2013). We have also upheld scraping underneath a suspect's fingernails to find evidence of a crime, calling that a "very limited intrusion." Cupp v. Murphy, 412 U.S. 291 (1973). A breath test is no more intrusive than either of these procedures.

Second, breath tests are capable of revealing only one bit of information, the amount of alcohol in the subject's breath. In this respect, they contrast sharply with the sample of cells collected by the swab in Maryland v. King. Although the DNA obtained under the law at issue in that case could lawfully be used only for identification purposes, the process put into the possession of law enforcement authorities a sample from which a wealth of additional, highly personal information could potentially be obtained. A breath test, by contrast, results in a BAC reading on a machine, nothing more. No sample of anything is left in the possession of the police.

Finally, participation in a breath test is not an experience that is likely to cause any great enhancement in the embarrassment that is inherent in any arrest. The act of blowing into a straw is not inherently embarrassing, nor are evidentiary breath tests administered in a manner that causes embarrassment. Again, such tests are normally administered in private at a police station, in a patrol car, or in a mobile testing facility, out of public view. Moreover, once placed under arrest, the individual's expectation of privacy is necessarily diminished. For all these reasons, we reiterate what we said in *Skinner*: A breath test does not implicate "significant privacy concerns."

Blood tests are a different matter. They "require piercing the skin" and extract a part of the subject's body. And while humans exhale air from their lungs many times per minute, humans do not continually shed blood. It is true, of course, that people voluntarily submit to the taking of blood samples as part of a physical examination, and the process involves little pain or risk. Nevertheless, for many, the process is not one they relish. It is significantly more intrusive than blowing into a tube. Perhaps that is why many States' implied consent laws, including Minnesota's, specifically prescribe that breath tests be administered in the usual drunk-driving case instead of blood tests or give motorists a measure of choice over which test to take.

In addition, a blood test, unlike a breath test, places in the hands of law enforcement authorities a sample that can be preserved and from which it is possible to extract information beyond a simple BAC reading. Even if the law enforcement agency is precluded from testing the blood for any purpose other than to measure BAC, the potential remains and may result in anxiety for the person tested.

Having assessed the impact of breath and blood testing on privacy interests, we now look to the States' asserted need to obtain BAC readings for persons arrested for drunk driving.

The States and the Federal Government have a paramount interest in preserving the safety of public highways. . . . Alcohol consumption is a leading cause of traffic fatalities and injuries. During the past decade, annual fatalities in drunk-driving accidents ranged from 13,582 deaths in 2005 to 9,865 deaths in 2011. . . . The laws at issue in the present cases—which make it a crime to refuse to submit to a BAC test—are designed to provide an incentive to cooperate in such cases, and we conclude that they serve a very important function. . . .

If a search warrant were required for every search incident to arrest that does not involve exigent circumstances, the courts would be swamped. And even if we arbitrarily singled out BAC tests incident to arrest for this special treatment, as it appears the dissent would do, the impact on the courts would be considerable. The number of arrests every year for driving under the influence is enormous—more than 1.1 million in 2014. Particularly in sparsely populated areas, it would be no small task for courts to field a large new influx of warrant applications that could come on any day of the year and at any hour. In many jurisdictions, judicial officers have the authority to issue warrants only within their own districts, and in rural areas, some districts may have only a small number of judicial officers.

North Dakota, for instance, has only 51 state district judges spread across eight judicial districts. Those judges are assisted by 31 magistrates, and there are no magistrates in 20 of the State's 53 counties. At any given location in the State, then, relatively few state officials have authority to issue search warrants. Yet the State, with a population of roughly 740,000, sees nearly 7,000 drunk-driving arrests each year. Office of North Dakota Attorney General, Crime in North Dakota, 2014, pp. 5, 47 (2015). . . .

In light of this burden and our prior search-incident-to-arrest precedents, petitioners would at a minimum have to show some special need for warrants for BAC testing. It is therefore appropriate to consider the benefits that such applications would provide. Search warrants protect privacy in two main ways. First, they ensure that a search is not carried out unless a neutral magistrate makes an independent determination that there is probable cause to believe that evidence will be found. Second, if the magistrate finds probable cause, the warrant limits the intrusion on privacy by specifying the scope of the search—that is, the area that can be searched and the items that can be sought.

How well would these functions be performed by the warrant applications that petitioners propose? In order to persuade a magistrate that there is probable cause for a search warrant, the officer would typically recite the same facts that led the officer to find that there was probable cause for arrest, namely, that there is probable cause to believe that a BAC test will reveal that the motorist's blood alcohol level is over the limit. As these three cases suggest, the facts that establish probable cause are largely the same from one drunk-driving stop to the next and consist largely of the officer's own characterization of his or her observations—for example, that there was a strong odor of alcohol, that the motorist wobbled when attempting to stand, that the motorist paused when reciting the alphabet or counting backwards, and so on. A magistrate would be in a poor position to challenge such characterizations.

As for the second function served by search warrants—delineating the scope of a search—the warrants in question here would not serve that function at all. In every case the scope of the warrant would simply be a BAC test of the arrestee. For these reasons, requiring the police to obtain a warrant in every case would impose a substantial burden but no commensurate benefit. . . .

Having assessed the effect of BAC tests on privacy interests and the need for such tests, we conclude that the Fourth Amendment permits warrantless breath tests incident to arrests for drunk driving. The impact of breath tests on privacy is slight, and the need for BAC testing is great.

We reach a different conclusion with respect to blood tests. Blood tests are significantly more intrusive, and their reasonableness must be judged in light of the availability of the less invasive alternative of a breath test. . . .

One advantage of blood tests is their ability to detect not just alcohol but also other substances that can impair a driver's ability to operate a car safely. A breath test cannot do this, but police have other measures at their disposal when they have reason to believe that a motorist may be under the influence of some other substance (for example, if a breath test indicates that a clearly impaired motorist has little if any alcohol in his blood). Nothing prevents the police from seeking a warrant for a blood test when there is sufficient time to do so in the particular circumstances or from relying on the exigent circumstances exception to the warrant requirement when there is not.

A blood test also requires less driver participation than a breath test. In order for a technician to take a blood sample, all that is needed is for the subject to remain still, either voluntarily or by being immobilized. Thus, it is possible to extract a blood sample from a subject who forcibly resists, but many States reasonably prefer not to take this step. North Dakota, for example, tells us that it generally opposes this practice because of the risk of dangerous altercations between police officers and arrestees in rural areas where the arresting officer may not have backup. Under current North Dakota law, only in cases involving an accident that results in death or serious injury may blood be taken from arrestees who resist.

It is true that a blood test, unlike a breath test, may be administered to a person who is unconscious (perhaps as a result of a crash) or who is unable to do what is needed to take a breath test due to profound intoxication or injuries. But we have no reason to believe that such situations are common in drunk-driving arrests, and when they arise, the police may apply for a warrant if need be. . . .

Because breath tests are significantly less intrusive than blood tests and in most cases amply serve law enforcement interests, we conclude that a breath test, but not a blood test, may be administered as a search incident to a lawful arrest for drunk driving. As in all cases involving reasonable searches incident to arrest, a warrant is not needed in this situation. . . .

Our remaining task is to apply our legal conclusions to the three cases before us. Petitioner Birchfield was criminally prosecuted for refusing a warrantless blood draw, and therefore the search he refused cannot be justified as a search incident to his arrest or on the basis of implied consent. There is no indication in the record or briefing that a breath test would have failed to satisfy the State's interests in acquiring evidence to enforce its drunk-driving laws against Birchfield. And North Dakota has not presented any case-specific information to suggest that the exigent circumstances exception would have justified a warrantless search. Unable to see any other basis on which to justify a warrantless test of Birchfield's blood, we conclude that Birchfield was threatened with an unlawful search and that the judgment affirming his conviction must be reversed. . . .

SOTOMAYOR, J., concurring in part and dissenting part.*

. . . I join the majority's disposition of *Birchfield* and *Beylun*, in which the Court holds that the search-incident-to-arrest exception to the Fourth Amendment's warrant requirement does not permit warrantless blood tests. But I dissent from the Court's disposition of *Bernard*, in which the Court holds that the same exception permits warrantless breath tests. Because no governmental interest categorically makes it impractical for an officer to obtain a warrant before measuring a driver's alcohol level, the Fourth Amendment prohibits such searches without a warrant, unless exigent circumstances exist in a particular case. . . .

A citizen's Fourth Amendment right to be free from "unreasonable searches" does not disappear upon arrest. Police officers may want to conduct a range of searches after placing a person under arrest. They may want to pat the arrestee down, search her pockets and purse, peek inside her wallet, scroll through her cellphone, examine her car or dwelling, swab her cheeks, or take blood and breath samples to determine her level of intoxication. But an officer is not authorized to conduct all of these searches simply because he has arrested someone. Each search must be separately analyzed to determine its reasonableness.

[The] question is whether, in light of the individual's privacy, a "legitimate governmental interest" justifies warrantless searches—and, if so, whether that governmental interest is adequately addressed by a case-

---

* [Justice Ginsburg joined this opinion—EDS.]

by-case exception or requires by its nature a categorical exception to the warrant requirement. The States . . . seek to exempt breath tests from the warrant requirement categorically under the search-incident-to-arrest doctrine. The majority agrees. Both are wrong. . . .

There is a common misconception that breath tests are conducted roadside, immediately after a driver is arrested. While some preliminary testing is conducted roadside, reliability concerns with roadside tests confine their use in most circumstances to establishing probable cause for an arrest. The standard evidentiary breath test is conducted after a motorist is arrested and transported to a police station, governmental building, or mobile testing facility where officers can access reliable, evidence-grade breath testing machinery. Transporting the motorist to the equipment site is not the only potential delay in the process, however. Officers must also observe the subject for 15 to 20 minutes to ensure that "residual mouth alcohol," which can inflate results and expose the test to an evidentiary challenge at trial, has dissipated and that the subject has not inserted any food or drink into his mouth. In many States, including Minnesota, officers must then give the motorist a window of time within which to contact an attorney before administering a test. Finally, if a breath test machine is not already active, the police officer must set it up. North Dakota's Intoxilyzer 8000 machine can take as long as 30 minutes to "warm-up."

Because of these necessary steps, the standard breath test is conducted well after an arrest is effectuated. . . . Both North Dakota and Minnesota give police a 2-hour period from the time the motorist was pulled over within which to administer a breath test. During this built-in window, police can seek warrants. That is particularly true in light of "advances" in technology that now permit "the more expeditious processing of warrant applications."

[The] States cite a governmental interest in minimizing the costs of gathering evidence of drunk driving. But neither has demonstrated that requiring police to obtain warrants for breath tests would impose a sufficiently significant burden on state resources to justify the elimination of the Fourth Amendment's warrant requirement. . . .

The Court notes that North Dakota has 82 judges and magistrate judges who are authorized to issue warrants. Because North Dakota has roughly 7,000 drunk-driving arrests annually, the Court concludes that if police were required to obtain warrants "for every search incident to arrest that does not involve exigent circumstances, the courts would be swamped." That conclusion relies on inflated numbers and unsupported inferences.

Assuming that North Dakota police officers do not obtain warrants for any drunk-driving arrests today, and assuming that they would need to obtain a warrant for every drunk-driving arrest tomorrow, each of the State's 82 judges and magistrate judges would need to issue fewer than two extra warrants per week. Minnesota has nearly the same ratio of judges to drunk-driving arrests, and so would face roughly the same burden. These back-of-the-envelope numbers suggest that the burden of obtaining a warrant before conducting a breath test would be small in both States.

But even these numbers *overstate* the burden by a significant degree. States only need to obtain warrants for drivers who refuse testing and a significant majority of drivers voluntarily consent to breath tests, even in States without criminal penalties for refusal. In North Dakota, only 21% of people refuse breath tests and in Minnesota, only 12% refuse. Including States that impose only *civil* penalties for refusal, the average refusal rate is slightly higher at 24%. Say that North Dakota's and Minnesota's refusal rates rise to double the mean, or 48%. Each of their judges and magistrate judges would need to issue fewer than one extra warrant a week. That bears repeating: The Court finds a categorical exception to the warrant requirement because each of a State's judges and magistrate judges would need to issue less than one extra warrant a week. . . .

This Court has never said that mere convenience in gathering evidence justifies an exception to the warrant requirement. If the simple collection of evidence justifies an exception to the warrant requirement even where a warrant could be easily obtained, exceptions would become the rule. . . .

In Maryland v. King, this Court dispensed with the warrant requirement and allowed DNA searches following an arrest. But there, it at least attempted to justify the search using the booking exception's interest in identifying arrestees. 569 U.S., at ___. Here, the Court lacks even the pretense of attempting to situate breath searches within the narrow and weighty law enforcement needs that have historically justified the limited use of warrantless searches. I fear that if the Court continues down this road, the Fourth Amendment's warrant requirement will become nothing more than a suggestion.

THOMAS, J., concurring in judgment in part, dissenting in part.

The compromise the Court reaches today is not a good one. By deciding that some (but not all) warrantless tests revealing the blood alcohol concentration (BAC) of an arrested driver are constitutional, the Court contorts the search-incident-to-arrest exception to the Fourth Amendment's warrant requirement. . . . The better (and far simpler) way to resolve these cases is by applying the *per se* rule that I proposed in *McNeely*. Under that approach, both warrantless breath and blood tests are constitutional because "the natural metabolization of [BAC] creates an exigency once police have probable cause to believe the driver is drunk. It naturally follows that police may conduct a search in these circumstances."

B. "Houses" and Other Places

1. The Outer Boundaries of Houses

Page 260. Add this material at the end of note 2.

See Collins v. Virginia, 138 S. Ct. 1663 (2018) (officer conducted improper warrantless search by entering curtilage of home to look under tarp for closer inspection of inspection of motorcycle; automobile exception does not permit the warrantless entry of curtilage to search a vehicle).

D. "Effects"

1. Inventory Searches

Page 298. Add this material at the end of note 2.

See also State v. Leak, 47 N.E.3d 821 (Ohio 2016) (no justification to impound and search a legally parked vehicle even though police arrested passenger on outstanding domestic violence warrant).

2. Cars and Containers

Page 316. Add this material at the end of note 4.

See also State v. Witt, 126 A.3d 850 (N.J. 2015) (changing state rule, officer who develops probable cause to search during the course of an unplanned vehicle stop no longer needs a warrant before conducting an on-scene search).

Chapter 5

Arrests

D. Paper Arrests: Citations

Page 352. Add this material at the end of note 2.

For an empirical exploration of citation practices, see International Association of Chiefs of Police, Citation in Lieu of Arrest: Examining Law Enforcement's Use of Citation Across the United States (April 2016), available at http://www.iacp.org/citation (concluding that 87% of agencies engaged in practice; agencies are using citation for nearly a third of all incidents, most often for disorderly conduct, theft, trespassing, driving under suspension, and possession of marijuana cases).

E. Use of Force in Making Arrests

Page 363. Add this material at the end of note 2.

In County of Los Angeles v. Mendez, 137 S. Ct. 1539 (2017), two deputies were searching for a parolee when they opened the door of a shack behind a residence, without a warrant and without knocking. Two men lived inside the shack, and one displayed a BB gun that he used to kill pests; the deputies saw the weapon and fired, injuring both men. When they sued under 42 U.S.C. § 1983 for excessive use of force, the

Ninth Circuit declared the claim viable because the deputies "intentionally or recklessly" provoked a violent confrontation when they committed an independent Fourth Amendment violation with their warrantless entry. The Supreme Court, however, declared that the Fourth Amendment provides no basis for such a "provocation" doctrine. The relevant constitutional question relates only to the reasonableness of the deputies' use of force, not the search and seizure violations that preceded that use of force.

Page 368. Add this material at the end of note 1.

See also Brandon L. Garrett & Seth W. Stoughton, A Tactical Fourth Amendment, 102 Va. L. Rev. 211 (2017) (empirical analysis of the force policies of the 50 largest policing agencies in the United States, finding that many agencies lacked guidance on the need to provide verbal warnings before using force, but noting a consistent approach among prominent agencies that adopt detailed policies, incorporating tactical methods to de-escalate and minimize the need to use force); Chad Flanders & Joseph C. Welling, Police Use of Deadly Force: State Statues 30 Years after Garner, St. Louis U. L.J. Online (Jan. 15, 2016), http://www.slu.edu/colleges/law/journal/police-use-of-deadly-force-state-statues-30-years-after-garner/. For an open-source database of police use of force policies, see http://useofforceproject.org/database/.

Chapter 6

Remedies for Unreasonable Searches and Seizures

B. Limitations on the Exclusionary Rule

2. Causation Limits

Page 401. Replace *Wehrenberg* with the following material.

Utah v. Edward Joseph Strieff, Jr.
579 U.S. ___ (2016)

THOMAS, J.*

To enforce the Fourth Amendment's prohibition against "unreasonable searches and seizures," this Court has at times required courts to exclude evidence obtained by unconstitutional police conduct. But the Court has also held that, even when there is a Fourth Amendment violation, this exclusionary rule does not apply when the costs of

* [Chief Justice Robert and Justices Kennedy, Breyer, and Alito joined this opinion—EDS.]

exclusion outweigh its deterrent benefits. In some cases, for example, the link between the unconstitutional conduct and the discovery of the evidence is too attenuated to justify suppression. The question in this case is whether this attenuation doctrine applies when an officer makes an unconstitutional investigatory stop; learns during that stop that the suspect is subject to a valid arrest warrant; and proceeds to arrest the suspect and seize incriminating evidence during a search incident to that arrest. We hold that the evidence the officer seized as part of the search incident to arrest is admissible because the officer's discovery of the arrest warrant attenuated the connection between the unlawful stop and the evidence seized incident to arrest.

This case began with an anonymous tip. In December 2006, someone called the South Salt Lake City police's drug-tip line to report "narcotics activity" at a particular residence. Narcotics detective Douglas Fackrell investigated the tip. Over the course of about a week, Officer Fackrell conducted intermittent surveillance of the home. He observed visitors who left a few minutes after arriving at the house. These visits were sufficiently frequent to raise his suspicion that the occupants were dealing drugs.

One of those visitors was respondent Edward Strieff. Officer Fackrell observed Strieff exit the house and walk toward a nearby convenience store. In the store's parking lot, Officer Fackrell detained Strieff, identified himself, and asked Strieff what he was doing at the residence.

As part of the stop, Officer Fackrell requested Strieff's identification, and Strieff produced his Utah identification card. Officer Fackrell relayed Strieff's information to a police dispatcher, who reported that Strieff had an outstanding arrest warrant for a traffic violation. Officer Fackrell then arrested Strieff pursuant to that warrant. When Officer Fackrell searched Strieff incident to the arrest, he discovered a baggie of methamphetamine and drug paraphernalia.

The State charged Strieff with unlawful possession of methamphetamine and drug paraphernalia. Strieff moved to suppress the evidence, arguing that the evidence was inadmissible because it was derived from an unlawful investigatory stop. At the suppression hearing, the prosecutor conceded that Officer Fackrell lacked reasonable suspicion for the stop but argued that the evidence should not be suppressed because the existence of a valid arrest warrant attenuated the connection between the unlawful stop and the discovery of the contraband.

The trial court agreed with the State and admitted the evidence. The court found that the short time between the illegal stop and the search weighed in favor of suppressing the evidence, but that two countervailing considerations made it admissible. First, the court considered the presence of a valid arrest warrant to be an "extraordinary intervening circumstance." Second, the court stressed the absence of flagrant misconduct by Officer Fackrell, who was conducting a legitimate investigation of a suspected drug house.

Strieff conditionally pleaded guilty to reduced charges of attempted possession of a controlled substance and possession of drug paraphernalia, but reserved his right to appeal the trial court's denial of the suppression motion. [The Utah Court of Appeals affirmed, but the Utah Supreme Court reversed, holding that] the evidence was inadmissible because only "a voluntary act of a defendant's free will (as in a confession or consent to search)" sufficiently breaks the connection between an illegal search and the discovery of evidence. . . . We granted certiorari to resolve disagreement about how the attenuation doctrine applies where an unconstitutional detention leads to the discovery of a valid arrest warrant. We now reverse.

The Fourth Amendment protects "[t]he right of the people to be secure in their persons, houses, papers, and effects, against unreasonable searches and seizures." Because officers who violated the Fourth Amendment were traditionally considered trespassers, individuals subject to unconstitutional searches or seizures historically enforced their rights through tort suits or self-help. Davies, Recovering the Original Fourth Amendment, 98 Mich. L. Rev. 547, 625 (1999). In the 20th century, however, the exclusionary rule—the rule that often requires trial courts to exclude unlawfully seized evidence in a criminal trial—became the principal judicial remedy to deter Fourth Amendment violations. See, e.g., Mapp v. Ohio, 367 U.S. 643 (1961).

Under the Court's precedents, the exclusionary rule encompasses both the "primary evidence obtained as a direct result of an illegal search or seizure" and, relevant here, "evidence later discovered and found to be derivative of an illegality," the so-called "fruit of the poisonous tree." Segura v. United States, 468 U.S. 796, 804 (1984). But the significant costs of this rule have led us to deem it "applicable only . . . where its deterrence benefits outweigh its substantial social costs." Hudson v.

Michigan, 547 U.S. 586 (2006). Suppression of evidence has always been our last resort, not our first impulse.

We have accordingly recognized several exceptions to the rule. Three of these exceptions involve the causal relationship between the unconstitutional act and the discovery of evidence. First, the independent source doctrine allows trial courts to admit evidence obtained in an unlawful search if officers independently acquired it from a separate, independent source. See Murray v. United States, 487 U.S. 533, 537 (1988). Second, the inevitable discovery doctrine allows for the admission of evidence that would have been discovered even without the unconstitutional source. See Nix v. Williams, 467 U.S. 431 (1984). Third, and at issue here, is the attenuation doctrine: Evidence is admissible when the connection between unconstitutional police conduct and the evidence is remote or has been interrupted by some intervening circumstance, so that "the interest protected by the constitutional guarantee that has been violated would not be served by suppression of the evidence obtained."

Turning to the application of the attenuation doctrine to this case, we first address a threshold question: whether this doctrine applies at all to a case like this, where the intervening circumstance that the State relies on is the discovery of a valid, pre-existing, and untainted arrest warrant. The Utah Supreme Court declined to apply the attenuation doctrine because it read our precedents as applying the doctrine only "to circumstances involving an independent act of a defendant's 'free will' in confessing to a crime or consenting to a search." In this Court, Strieff has not defended this argument, and we disagree with it, as well. The attenuation doctrine evaluates the causal link between the government's unlawful act and the discovery of evidence, which often has nothing to do with a defendant's actions. And the logic of our prior attenuation cases is not limited to independent acts by the defendant.

It remains for us to address whether the discovery of a valid arrest warrant was a sufficient intervening event to break the causal chain between the unlawful stop and the discovery of drug-related evidence on Strieff's person. The three factors articulated in Brown v. Illinois, 422 U.S. 590 (1975), guide our analysis. First, we look to the "temporal proximity" between the unconstitutional conduct and the discovery of evidence to determine how closely the discovery of evidence followed the unconstitutional search. Second, we consider "the presence of intervening circumstances." Third, and "particularly" significant, we examine "the purpose and flagrancy of the official misconduct." In evaluating these factors, we assume without deciding (because the State conceded the point) that Officer Fackrell lacked reasonable suspicion to initially stop Strieff. And, because we ultimately conclude that the warrant breaks the causal chain, we also have no need to decide whether the warrant's existence alone would make the initial stop constitutional even if Officer Fackrell was unaware of its existence.

The first factor, temporal proximity between the initially unlawful stop and the search, favors suppressing the evidence. Our precedents have declined to find that this factor favors attenuation unless "substantial time" elapses between an unlawful act and when the evidence is obtained. Here, however, Officer Fackrell discovered drug contraband on Strieff's person only minutes after the illegal stop. As the Court explained in *Brown,* such a short time interval counsels in favor of suppression; there, we found that the confession should be suppressed, relying in part on the "less than two hours" that separated the unconstitutional arrest and the confession.

In contrast, the second factor, the presence of intervening circumstances, strongly favors the State. In *Segura,* the Court addressed similar facts to those here and found sufficient intervening circumstances to allow the admission of evidence. There, agents had probable cause to believe that apartment occupants were dealing cocaine. They sought a warrant. In the meantime, they entered the apartment, arrested an occupant, and discovered evidence of drug activity during a limited search for security reasons. The next evening, the Magistrate Judge issued the search warrant. This Court deemed the evidence admissible notwithstanding the illegal search because the information supporting the warrant was "wholly unconnected with the [arguably illegal] entry and was known to the agents well before the initial entry."

Segura, of course, applied the independent source doctrine because the unlawful entry "did not contribute in any way to discovery of the evidence seized under the warrant." But the *Segura* Court suggested that the existence of a valid warrant favors finding that the connection between unlawful conduct and the discovery of evidence is "sufficiently attenuated to dissipate the taint." That principle applies here.

In this case, the warrant was valid, it predated Officer Fackrell's investigation, and it was entirely unconnected with the stop. And once Officer Fackrell discovered the warrant, he had an obligation to arrest

Strieff. "A warrant is a judicial mandate to an officer to conduct a search or make an arrest, and the officer has a sworn duty to carry out its provisions." United States v. Leon, 468 U.S. 897 (1984). Officer Fackrell's arrest of Strieff thus was a ministerial act that was independently compelled by the pre-existing warrant. And once Officer Fackrell was authorized to arrest Strieff, it was undisputedly lawful to search Strieff as an incident of his arrest to protect Officer Fackrell's safety.

Finally, the third factor, "the purpose and flagrancy of the official misconduct," also strongly favors the State. The exclusionary rule exists to deter police misconduct. The third factor of the attenuation doctrine reflects that rationale by favoring exclusion only when the police misconduct is most in need of deterrence—that is, when it is purposeful or flagrant.

Officer Fackrell was at most negligent. In stopping Strieff, Officer Fackrell made two good-faith mistakes. First, he had not observed what time Strieff entered the suspected drug house, so he did not know how long Strieff had been there. Officer Fackrell thus lacked a sufficient basis to conclude that Strieff was a short-term visitor who may have been consummating a drug transaction. Second, because he lacked confirmation that Strieff was a short-term visitor, Officer Fackrell should have asked Strieff whether he would speak with him, instead of demanding that Strieff do so. Officer Fackrell's stated purpose was to "find out what was going on [in] the house." Nothing prevented him from approaching Strieff simply to ask. But these errors in judgment hardly rise to a purposeful or flagrant violation of Strieff's Fourth Amendment rights.

While Officer Fackrell's decision to initiate the stop was mistaken, his conduct thereafter was lawful. The officer's decision to run the warrant check was a negligibly burdensome precaution for officer safety. And Officer Fackrell's actual search of Strieff was a lawful search incident to arrest.

Moreover, there is no indication that this unlawful stop was part of any systemic or recurrent police misconduct. To the contrary, all the evidence suggests that the stop was an isolated instance of negligence that occurred in connection with a bona fide investigation of a suspected drug house. Officer Fackrell saw Strieff leave a suspected drug house. And his suspicion about the house was based on an anonymous tip and his personal observations.

Applying these factors, we hold that the evidence discovered on Strieff's person was admissible because the unlawful stop was sufficiently attenuated by the pre-existing arrest warrant. Although the illegal stop was close in time to Strieff's arrest, that consideration is outweighed by two factors supporting the State. The outstanding arrest warrant for Strieff's arrest is a critical intervening circumstance that is wholly independent of the illegal stop. The discovery of that warrant broke the causal chain between the unconstitutional stop and the discovery of evidence by compelling Officer Fackrell to arrest Strieff. And, it is especially significant that there is no evidence that Officer Fackrell's illegal stop reflected flagrantly unlawful police misconduct.

We find Strieff's counterarguments unpersuasive.

First, he argues that the attenuation doctrine should not apply because the officer's stop was purposeful and flagrant. He asserts that Officer Fackrell stopped him solely to fish for evidence of suspected wrongdoing. But Officer Fackrell sought information from Strieff to find out what was happening inside a house whose occupants were legitimately suspected of dealing drugs. This was not a suspicionless fishing expedition "in the hope that something would turn up."

Strieff argues, moreover, that Officer Fackrell's conduct was flagrant because he detained Strieff without the necessary level of cause (here, reasonable suspicion). But that conflates the standard for an illegal stop with the standard for flagrancy. For the violation to be flagrant, more severe police misconduct is required than the mere absence of proper cause for the seizure. Neither the officer's alleged purpose nor the flagrancy of the violation rise to a level of misconduct to warrant suppression.

Second, Strieff argues that, because of the prevalence of outstanding arrest warrants in many jurisdictions, police will engage in dragnet searches if the exclusionary rule is not applied. We think that this outcome is unlikely. Such wanton conduct would expose police to civil liability. See 42 U.S.C. § 1983; Monell v. New York City Dept. of Social Servs., 436 U.S. 658, 690 (1978). And in any event, the Brown factors take account of the purpose and flagrancy of police misconduct. Were evidence of a dragnet search presented here, the application of the *Brown* factors could be different. But there is no evidence that the concerns that Strieff raises with the criminal justice system are present in South Salt Lake City, Utah.

We hold that the evidence Officer Fackrell seized as part of his search incident to arrest is admissible because his discovery of the arrest warrant attenuated the connection between the unlawful stop and the evidence seized from Strieff incident to arrest. The judgment of the Utah Supreme Court, accordingly, is reversed.

SOTOMAYOR, J., dissenting.*

The Court today holds that the discovery of a warrant for an unpaid parking ticket will forgive a police officer's violation of your Fourth Amendment rights. Do not be soothed by the opinion's technical language: This case allows the police to stop you on the street, demand your identification, and check it for outstanding traffic warrants—even if you are doing nothing wrong. If the officer discovers a warrant for a fine you forgot to pay, courts will now excuse his illegal stop and will admit into evidence anything he happens to find by searching you after arresting you on the warrant. Because the Fourth Amendment should prohibit, not permit, such misconduct, I dissent.

Minutes after Edward Strieff walked out of a South Salt Lake City home, an officer stopped him, questioned him, and took his identification to run it through a police database. The officer did not suspect that Strieff had done anything wrong. Strieff just happened to be the first person to leave a house that the officer thought might contain "drug activity."

As the State of Utah concedes, this stop was illegal. The Fourth Amendment protects people from "unreasonable searches and seizures." An officer breaches that protection when he detains a pedestrian to check his license without any evidence that the person is engaged in a crime. The officer deepens the breach when he prolongs the detention just to fish further for evidence of wrongdoing. In his search for lawbreaking, the officer in this case himself broke the law.

The officer learned that Strieff had a "small traffic warrant." Pursuant to that warrant, he arrested Strieff and, conducting a search incident to the arrest, discovered methamphetamine in Strieff's pockets. . . .

It is tempting in a case like this, where illegal conduct by an officer uncovers illegal conduct by a civilian, to forgive the officer. After all, his instincts, although unconstitutional, were correct. But a basic principle lies at the heart of the Fourth Amendment: Two wrongs don't make a

---

* [Justice Ginsburg joined Parts I through III of this opinion—EDS.]

right. See Weeks v. United States, 232 U.S. 383, 392 (1914). When "lawless police conduct" uncovers evidence of lawless civilian conduct, this Court has long required later criminal trials to exclude the illegally obtained evidence. For example, if an officer breaks into a home and finds a forged check lying around, that check may not be used to prosecute the homeowner for bank fraud. We would describe the check as "fruit of the poisonous tree." Fruit that must be cast aside includes not only evidence directly found by an illegal search but also evidence "come at by exploitation of that illegality."

This "exclusionary rule" removes an incentive for officers to search us without proper justification. It also keeps courts from being "made party to lawless invasions of the constitutional rights of citizens by permitting unhindered governmental use of the fruits of such invasions." When courts admit only lawfully obtained evidence, they encourage "those who formulate law enforcement polices, and the officers who implement them, to incorporate Fourth Amendment ideals into their value system." But when courts admit illegally obtained evidence as well, they reward "manifest neglect if not an open defiance of the prohibitions of the Constitution."

Applying the exclusionary rule, the Utah Supreme Court correctly decided that Strieff's drugs must be excluded because the officer exploited his illegal stop to discover them. The officer found the drugs only after learning of Strieff's traffic violation; and he learned of Strieff's traffic violation only because he unlawfully stopped Strieff to check his driver's license.

The court also correctly rejected the State's argument that the officer's discovery of a traffic warrant unspoiled the poisonous fruit. The State analogizes finding the warrant to one of our earlier decisions, Wong Sun v. United States, 371 U.S. 471 (1963). There, an officer illegally arrested a person who, days later, voluntarily returned to the station to confess to committing a crime. Even though the person would not have confessed "but for the illegal actions of the police," we noted that the police did not exploit their illegal arrest to obtain the confession. Because the confession was obtained by "means sufficiently distinguishable" from the constitutional violation, we held that it could be admitted into evidence. The State contends that the search incident to the warrant-arrest here is similarly distinguishable from the illegal stop.

But *Wong Sun* explains why Strieff's drugs must be excluded. We reasoned that a Fourth Amendment violation may not color every investigation that follows but it certainly stains the actions of officers who exploit the infraction. We distinguished evidence obtained by innocuous means from evidence obtained by exploiting misconduct after considering a variety of factors: whether a long time passed, whether there were "intervening circumstances," and whether the purpose or flagrancy of the misconduct was "calculated" to procure the evidence.

These factors confirm that the officer in this case discovered Strieff's drugs by exploiting his own illegal conduct. The officer did not ask Strieff to volunteer his name only to find out, days later, that Strieff had a warrant against him. The officer illegally stopped Strieff and immediately ran a warrant check. The officer's discovery of a warrant was not some intervening surprise that he could not have anticipated. Utah lists over 180,000 misdemeanor warrants in its database, and at the time of the arrest, Salt Lake County had a backlog of outstanding warrants so large that it faced the "potential for civil liability." See Dept. of Justice, Bureau of Justice Statistics, Survey of State Criminal History Information Systems, 2014 (2015) (Systems Survey) (Table 5a), online at https://www.ncjrs.gov/pdffiles1/bjs/grants/249799.pdf. The officer's violation was also calculated to procure evidence. His sole reason for stopping Strieff, he acknowledged, was investigative—he wanted to discover whether drug activity was going on in the house Strieff had just exited.

The warrant check, in other words, was not an "intervening circumstance" separating the stop from the search for drugs. It was part and parcel of the officer's illegal "expedition for evidence in the hope that something might turn up." Under our precedents, because the officer found Strieff's drugs by exploiting his own constitutional violation, the drugs should be excluded.

The Court sees things differently. To the Court, the fact that a warrant gives an officer cause to arrest a person severs the connection between illegal policing and the resulting discovery of evidence. This is a remarkable proposition: The mere existence of a warrant not only gives an officer legal cause to arrest and search a person, it also forgives an officer who, with no knowledge of the warrant at all, unlawfully stops that person on a whim or hunch. . . .

The majority likewise misses the point when it calls the warrant check here a "negligibly burdensome precaution" taken for the officer's "safety." Remember, the officer stopped Strieff without suspecting him of committing any crime. By his own account, the officer did not fear Strieff. . . . Surely we would not allow officers to warrant-check random joggers, dog walkers, and lemonade vendors just to ensure they pose no threat to anyone else.

The majority also posits that the officer could not have exploited his illegal conduct because he did not violate the Fourth Amendment on purpose. Rather, he made "good-faith mistakes." Never mind that the officer's sole purpose was to fish for evidence. The majority casts his unconstitutional actions as "negligent" and therefore incapable of being deterred by the exclusionary rule.

But the Fourth Amendment does not tolerate an officer's unreasonable searches and seizures just because he did not know any better. Even officers prone to negligence can learn from courts that exclude illegally obtained evidence. Indeed, they are perhaps the most in need of the education, whether by the judge's opinion, the prosecutor's future guidance, or an updated manual on criminal procedure. If the officers are in doubt about what the law requires, exclusion gives them an "incentive to err on the side of constitutional behavior."

Most striking about the Court's opinion is its insistence that the event here was "isolated," with "no indication that this unlawful stop was part of any systemic or recurrent police misconduct." Respectfully, nothing about this case is isolated.

Outstanding warrants are surprisingly common. When a person with a traffic ticket misses a fine payment or court appearance, a court will issue a warrant. The States and Federal Government maintain databases with over 7.8 million outstanding warrants, the vast majority of which appear to be for minor offenses. Even these sources may not track the "staggering" numbers of warrants, "drawers and drawers" full, that many cities issue for traffic violations and ordinance infractions. Dept. of Justice, Civil Rights Div., Investigation of the Ferguson Police Department 47, 55 (2015) (Ferguson Report). The county in this case has had a "backlog" of such warrants. The Department of Justice recently reported that in the town of Ferguson, Missouri, with a population of 21,000, 16,000 people had outstanding warrants against them.

Justice Department investigations across the country have illustrated how these astounding numbers of warrants can be used by police to stop people without cause. In a single year in New Orleans, officers "made nearly 60,000 arrests, of which about 20,000 were of people with outstanding traffic or misdemeanor warrants from neighboring parishes for such infractions as unpaid tickets." Dept. of Justice, Civil Rights Div., Investigation of the New Orleans Police Department 29 (2011). In the St. Louis metropolitan area, officers "routinely" stop people—on the street, at bus stops, or even in court—for no reason other than "an officer's desire to check whether the subject had a municipal arrest warrant pending." Ferguson Report, at 49, 57. In Newark, New Jersey, officers stopped 52,235 pedestrians within a 4-year period and ran warrant checks on 39,308 of them. Dept. of Justice, Civil Rights Div., Investigation of the Newark Police Department 8, 19, n. 15 (2014). The Justice Department analyzed these warrant-checked stops and reported that "approximately 93% of the stops would have been considered unsupported by articulated reasonable suspicion."

I do not doubt that most officers act in "good faith" and do not set out to break the law. That does not mean these stops are "isolated instances of negligence," however. Many are the product of institutionalized training procedures. The New York City Police Department long trained officers to, in the words of a District Judge, "stop and question first, develop reasonable suspicion later." Ligon v. New York, 925 F. Supp. 2d 478, 537-538 (S.D.N.Y. 2013), stay granted on other grounds, 736 F.3d 118 (2d Cir. 2013). The Utah Supreme Court described as "routine procedure" or "common practice" the decision of Salt Lake City police officers to run warrant checks on pedestrians they detained without reasonable suspicion. State v. Topanotes, 76 P.3d 1159, 1160 (Utah 2003). In the related context of traffic stops, one widely followed police manual instructs officers looking for drugs to "run at least a warrants check on all drivers you stop. Statistically, narcotics offenders are . . . more likely to fail to appear on simple citations, such as traffic or trespass violations, leading to the issuance of bench warrants. Discovery of an outstanding warrant gives you cause for an immediate custodial arrest and search of the suspect." C. Remsberg, Tactics for Criminal Patrol 205-206 (1995); C. Epp et al., Pulled Over 23, 33-36 (2014).

The majority does not suggest what makes this case "isolated" from these and countless other examples. Nor does it offer guidance for how a defendant can prove that his arrest was the result of "widespread" misconduct. Surely it should not take a federal investigation of Salt Lake County before the Court would protect someone in Strieff's position.

Writing only for myself, and drawing on my professional

experiences, I would add that unlawful "stops" have severe consequences much greater than the inconvenience suggested by the name. This Court has given officers an array of instruments to probe and examine you. When we condone officers' use of these devices without adequate cause, we give them reason to target pedestrians in an arbitrary manner. We also risk treating members of our communities as second-class citizens.

Although many Americans have been stopped for speeding or jaywalking, few may realize how degrading a stop can be when the officer is looking for more. This Court has allowed an officer to stop you for whatever reason he wants—so long as he can point to a pretextual justification after the fact. Whren v. United States, 517 U.S. 806 (1996). That justification must provide specific reasons why the officer suspected you were breaking the law, but it may factor in your ethnicity, United States v. Brignoni-Ponce, 422 U.S. 873 (1975), where you live, Adams v. Williams, 407 U.S. 143 (1972), what you were wearing, United States v. Sokolow, 490 U.S. 1 (1989), and how you behaved, Illinois v. Wardlow, 528 U.S. 119 (2000). The officer does not even need to know which law you might have broken so long as he can later point to any possible infraction—even one that is minor, unrelated, or ambiguous. Devenpeck v. Alford, 543 U.S. 146 (2004); Heien v. North Carolina, 574 U.S. __ (2014).

The indignity of the stop is not limited to an officer telling you that you look like a criminal. The officer may next ask for your "consent" to inspect your bag or purse without telling you that you can decline. Regardless of your answer, he may order you to stand "helpless, perhaps facing a wall with [your] hands raised." If the officer thinks you might be dangerous, he may then "frisk" you for weapons. This involves more than just a pat down. As onlookers pass by, the officer may "feel with sensitive fingers every portion of [your] body. A thorough search [may] be made of [your] arms and armpits, waistline and back, the groin and area about the testicles, and entire surface of the legs down to the feet."

The officer's control over you does not end with the stop. If the officer chooses, he may handcuff you and take you to jail for doing nothing more than speeding, jaywalking, or "driving [your] pickup truck . . . with [your] 3-year-old son and 5-year-old daughter . . . without [your] seatbelt fastened." Atwater v. Lago Vista, 532 U.S. 318 (2001). At the jail, he can fingerprint you, swab DNA from the inside of your mouth, and force you to "shower with a delousing agent" while you "lift

[your] tongue, hold out [your] arms, turn around, and lift [your] genitals." Florence v. Board of Chosen Freeholders of County of Burlington, 566 U.S. ___ (2012); Maryland v. King, 569 U.S. ___ (2013). Even if you are innocent, you will now join the 65 million Americans with an arrest record and experience the "civil death" of discrimination by employers, landlords, and whoever else conducts a background check. Chin, The New Civil Death, 160 U. Pa. L. Rev. 1789, 1805 (2012); see J. Jacobs, The Eternal Criminal Record 33-51 (2015); Young & Petersilia, Keeping Track, 129 Harv. L. Rev. 1318 (2016). And, of course, if you fail to pay bail or appear for court, a judge will issue a warrant to render you "arrestable on sight" in the future. A. Goffman, On the Run 196 (2014).

This case involves a *suspicionless* stop, one in which the officer initiated this chain of events without justification. As the Justice Department notes, many innocent people are subjected to the humiliations of these unconstitutional searches. The white defendant in this case shows that anyone's dignity can be violated in this manner. But it is no secret that people of color are disproportionate victims of this type of scrutiny. See M. Alexander, The New Jim Crow 95-136 (2010). For generations, black and brown parents have given their children "the talk"—instructing them never to run down the street; always keep your hands where they can be seen; do not even think of talking back to a stranger—all out of fear of how an officer with a gun will react to them. See, *e.g.,* W.E.B. Du Bois, The Souls of Black Folk (1903); J. Baldwin, The Fire Next Time (1963); T. Coates, Between the World and Me (2015).

By legitimizing the conduct that produces this double consciousness, this case tells everyone, white and black, guilty and innocent, that an officer can verify your legal status at any time. It says that your body is subject to invasion while courts excuse the violation of your rights. It implies that you are not a citizen of a democracy but the subject of a carceral state, just waiting to be cataloged.

We must not pretend that the countless people who are routinely targeted by police are "isolated." They are the canaries in the coal mine whose deaths, civil and literal, warn us that no one can breathe in this atmosphere. See L. Guinier & G. Torres, The Miner's Canary 274-283 (2002). They are the ones who recognize that unlawful police stops corrode all our civil liberties and threaten all our lives. Until their voices matter too, our justice system will continue to be anything but.

KAGAN, J., dissenting.[*]

If a police officer stops a person on the street without reasonable suspicion, that seizure violates the Fourth Amendment. And if the officer pats down the unlawfully detained individual and finds drugs in his pocket, the State may not use the contraband as evidence in a criminal prosecution. That much is beyond dispute. The question here is whether the prohibition on admitting evidence dissolves if the officer discovers, after making the stop but before finding the drugs, that the person has an outstanding arrest warrant. Because that added wrinkle makes no difference under the Constitution, I respectfully dissent. . . .

[Consider] whether any intervening circumstance "broke the causal chain" between the stop and the evidence. The notion of such a disrupting event comes from the tort law doctrine of proximate causation. And as in the tort context, a circumstance counts as intervening only when it is unforeseeable—not when it can be seen coming from miles away. For rather than breaking the causal chain, predictable effects (*e.g.,* X leads naturally to Y leads naturally to Z) are its very links.

And Fackrell's discovery of an arrest warrant—the only event the majority thinks intervened—was an eminently foreseeable consequence of stopping Strieff. As Fackrell testified, checking for outstanding warrants during a stop is the "normal" practice of South Salt Lake City police. In other words, the department's standard detention procedures—stop, ask for identification, run a check—are partly designed to find outstanding warrants. And find them they will, given the staggering number of such warrants on the books. . . . They are the run-of-the-mill results of police stops—what officers look for when they run a routine check of a person's identification and what they know will turn up with fair regularity. In short, they are nothing like what intervening circumstances are supposed to be. . . .

The majority's misapplication of *Brown*'s three-part inquiry creates unfortunate incentives for the police—indeed, practically invites them to do what Fackrell did here. Consider an officer who, like Fackrell, wishes to stop someone for investigative reasons, but does not have what a court would view as reasonable suspicion. If the officer believes that any

---

[*] [Justice Ginsburg joined this opinion—EDS.]

evidence he discovers will be inadmissible, he is likely to think the unlawful stop not worth making—precisely the deterrence the exclusionary rule is meant to achieve. But when he is told of today's decision? Now the officer knows that the stop may well yield admissible evidence: So long as the target is one of the many millions of people in this country with an outstanding arrest warrant, anything the officer finds in a search is fair game for use in a criminal prosecution. The officer's incentive to violate the Constitution thus increases: From here on, he sees potential advantage in stopping individuals without reasonable suspicion—exactly the temptation the exclusionary rule is supposed to remove. Because the majority thus places Fourth Amendment protections at risk, I respectfully dissent.

Page 409. Add this material at the end of note 2.

See also Rodriguez v. State, 187 So. 3d 841 (Fla. 2015) (adopting minority position; marijuana found during a warrantless home intrusion isn't admissible under the inevitable-discovery exception to the exclusionary rule unless the police were already in the process of seeking a warrant to search the residence).

3. Standing to Challenge Illegal Searches and Seizures

Page 417. Add this material at the end of note 1.

See Byrd v. United States, 138 S. Ct. 1518 (2018) (fact that a driver in lawful possession or control of a rental car is not listed on the rental agreement will not, standing alone, defeat his or her otherwise reasonable expectation of privacy protected by the Fourth Amendment).

C. Additions and Alternatives to the Exclusionary Rule

2. Tort Actions and Criminal Prosecutions

Page 439. Add this material at the end of note 1.

It is possible for a defendant to file a civil suit for damages under 42 U.S.C. § 1983 based on a Fourth Amendment violation if a city detains the defendant improperly after the probable cause to support an arrest no longer exists. In Manuel v. City of Joliet, Illinois, 137 S. Ct. 911 (2017), police arrested a suspect on drug charges but the police laboratory determined that the pills found on the defendant contained no controlled substances. Nevertheless, the city detained Manuel for 48 days. The Supreme Court held that Manuel could challenge his pretrial detention on Fourth Amendment grounds in a civil action under Section 1983.

On the other hand, the U.S. Supreme Court has placed substantial new limits on *Bivens* actions. In Ziglar v. Abbasi, 137 S. Ct. 1843 (2017), non-citizens who were detained in the period after the September 11, 2001 attacks brought a civil damages action, alleging that their detention was unconstitutional. The Supreme Court affirmed the lower courts' dismissal of the claims. The opinion started with a new analytical framework for *Bivens* actions: when a party seeks to assert an implied cause of action under the Constitution, separation-of-powers principles should be central to the analysis. Most often, Congress should authorize any damages suit, and the courts not extend a right of action to a new context if there are "special factors" to counsel "hesitation." If there are sound reasons to think Congress "might doubt the efficacy or necessity" of a damages remedy, courts must refrain from creating that remedy. See also Hernandez v. Mesa, 137 S. Ct. 2003 (2017) (no *Bivens* action available for parents of a victim shot by a U.S. Border Patrol agent on Mexican soil).

Page 440. Add this material at the end of note 2.

Sharon Cohen, How Chicago Racked Up a $662 Million Police Misconduct Bill, Salon, Mar. 19, 2016, available at http://www.salon.com/2016/03/19/how_chicago_racked_up_a_662_million_police_misconduct_bill/.

Page 441. Add this material at the end of note 3.

See also District of Columbia v. Wesby, 138 S. Ct. 577 (2018) (officers entitled to qualified when they arrested partygoers in vacant house for unlawful entry and found circumstances to support their disbelief of partygoers' claim that lessee authorized their entry); City and County of San Francisco v. Sheehan, 135 S. Ct. 1765 (2015) (police officers who twice entered room of a woman with a mental disability and shot her without stopping to consider how to accommodate her mental illness were entitled to qualified immunity from civil lawsuit; first entry was legal, and there was no clearly established law requiring them to accommodate her mental illness before second entry); Mullenix v. Luna, 136 S. Ct. 305 (2015) (police officer who shot at a fleeing suspect's car was entitled to qualified immunity, unless existing precedent makes a conclusion of unreasonable action "beyond debate").

Chapter 7

Technology and Privacy

A. Enhancement of the Senses

Page 456. Add this material at the end of note 1.

See also Grady v. North Carolina, 135 S. Ct. 1368 (2015) (attachment of a satellite-based tracking device to the person of a recidivist sex offender qualifies as a "search" for purposes of the Fourth Amendment's reasonableness requirement); People v. Herrera, 357 P.3d 1227 (Colo. 2015) (police exceeded the scope of a search warrant authorizing them to examine a man's mobile phone for specified text messages and indicia of ownership when they began searching through unrelated files stored in the phone).

B. Wiretapping

Page 472. Add this material at the end of note 6.

See also Dahda v. United States, 138 S. Ct. 1491 (2018) (exclusion remedy not required because judicial order authorizing wiretap provided proper support for wiretap within jurisdictional boundaries; provision in order authorizing wiretaps outside jurisdictional boundaries was erroneous but did not render the order "facially" insufficient).

C. *Government Access to Databases*

Page 496. Add this material before the notes.

TIMOTHY IVORY CARPENTER v. UNITED STATES
2018 WL 3073916 (June 22, 2018)

ROBERTS, C.J.*

This case presents the question whether the Government conducts a search under the Fourth Amendment when it accesses historical cell phone records that provide a comprehensive chronicle of the user's past movements.

I.

A.

There are 396 million cell phone service accounts in the United States—for a Nation of 326 million people. Cell phones perform their wide and growing variety of functions by connecting to a set of radio antennas called "cell sites." Although cell sites are usually mounted on a tower, they can also be found on light posts, flagpoles, church steeples, or the sides of buildings. Cell sites typically have several directional antennas that divide the covered area into sectors.

Cell phones continuously scan their environment looking for the best signal, which generally comes from the closest cell site. Most modern devices, such as smartphones, tap into the wireless network several times a minute whenever their signal is on, even if the owner is not using one of the phone's features. Each time the phone connects to a cell site, it generates a time-stamped record known as cell-site location information (CSLI). The precision of this information depends on the size of the geographic area covered by the cell site. The greater the concentration of cell sites, the smaller the coverage area. As data usage from cell phones has increased, wireless carriers have installed more cell sites to handle the traffic. That has led to increasingly compact coverage areas, especially in urban areas.

Wireless carriers collect and store CSLI for their own business purposes, including finding weak spots in their network and applying "roaming" charges when another carrier routes data through their cell

---

* [Justices Ginsburg, Breyer, Sotomayor, and Kagan joined this opinion—EDS.]

sites. . . . While carriers have long retained CSLI for the start and end of incoming calls, in recent years phone companies have also collected location information from the transmission of text messages and routine data connections. Accordingly, modern cell phones generate increasingly vast amounts of increasingly precise CSLI.

B.

[Prosecutors suspected Timothy Carpenter and a group of fifteen accomplices of robbing a series of Radio Shack and T-Mobile stores in Detroit. Based on information received from one of the suspects, the prosecutors applied for court orders under the Stored Communications Act to obtain cell phone records for petitioner Carpenter and several other suspects.]

That statute, as amended in 1994, permits the Government to compel the disclosure of certain telecommunications records when it "offers specific and articulable facts showing that there are reasonable grounds to believe" that the records sought "are relevant and material to an ongoing criminal investigation." U.S.C. §2703(d). Federal Magistrate Judges issued two orders directing Carpenter's wireless carriers—MetroPCS and Sprint—to disclose "cell/site sector" information for Carpenter's telephone "at call origination and at call termination for incoming and outgoing calls" during the four-month period when the string of robberies occurred. The first order sought 152 days of cell-site records from MetroPCS, which produced records spanning 127 days. The second order requested seven days of CSLI from Sprint, which produced two days of records covering the period when Carpenter's phone was "roaming" in northeastern Ohio. Altogether the Government obtained 12,898 location points cataloging Carpenter's movements—an average of 101 data points per day.

[Before trial, Carpenter moved to suppress the cell site location data because it was obtained through a warrantless search based on a showing of reasonable suspicion rather than probable cause, but the trial court denied the motion. Based in part on the cell site location data, Carpenter was convicted of robbery and carrying a firearm during a federal crime of violence.]

II.

. . . We have kept [our] attention to Founding-era understandings in mind when applying the Fourth Amendment to innovations in surveillance tools. As technology has enhanced the Government's capacity to encroach upon areas normally guarded from inquisitive eyes, this Court has sought to assure preservation of "that degree of privacy against government that existed when the Fourth Amendment was adopted."

[Requests] for cell-site records lie at the intersection of two lines of cases, both of which inform our understanding of the privacy interests at stake. The first set of cases addresses a person's expectation of privacy in his physical location and movements. . . . In United States v. Jones, 565 U.S. 400 (2012), FBI agents installed a GPS tracking device on Jones's vehicle and remotely monitored the vehicle's movements for 28 days. The Court decided the case based on the Government's physical trespass of the vehicle. At the same time, five Justices agreed that related privacy concerns would be raised by, for example, "surreptitiously activating a stolen vehicle detection system" in Jones's car to track Jones himself, or conducting GPS tracking of his cell phone. . . . Since GPS monitoring of a vehicle tracks "every movement" a person makes in that vehicle, the concurring Justices concluded that "longer term GPS monitoring in investigations of most offenses impinges on expectations of privacy"—regardless whether those movements were disclosed to the public at large. . . .

In a second set of decisions, the Court has drawn a line between what a person keeps to himself and what he shares with others. We have previously held that "a person has no legitimate expectation of privacy in information he voluntarily turns over to third parties." Smith v. Maryland, 442 U. S. 735, 743-744 (1979). That remains true "even if the information is revealed on the assumption that it will be used only for a limited purpose." United States v. Miller, 425 U. S. 435, 443 (1976). As a result, the Government is typically free to obtain such information from the recipient without triggering Fourth Amendment protections. . . .

III.

The question we confront today is how to apply the Fourth Amendment to a new phenomenon: the ability to chronicle a person's past movements through the record of his cell phone signals. Such tracking partakes of many of the qualities of the GPS monitoring we considered in *Jones*. Much like GPS tracking of a vehicle, cell phone location information is detailed, encyclopedic, and effortlessly compiled.

At the same time, the fact that the individual continuously reveals his location to his wireless carrier implicates the third-party principle of *Smith* and *Miller*. But while the third-party doctrine applies to telephone numbers and bank records, it is not clear whether its logic extends to the qualitatively different category of cell-site records. After all, when *Smith* was decided in 1979, few could have imagined a society in which a phone goes wherever its owner goes, conveying to the wireless carrier not just dialed digits, but a detailed and comprehensive record of the person's movements.

We decline to extend *Smith* and *Miller* to cover these novel circumstances. Given the unique nature of cellphone location records, the fact that the information is held by a third party does not by itself overcome the user's claim to Fourth Amendment protection. Whether the Government employs its own surveillance technology as in *Jones* or leverages the technology of a wireless carrier, we hold that an individual maintains a legitimate expectation of privacy in the record of his physical movements as captured through CSLI. The location information obtained from Carpenter's wireless carriers was the product of a search.[3]

A.

A person does not surrender all Fourth Amendment protection by venturing into the public sphere. To the contrary, what one seeks to "preserve as private, even in an area accessible to the public, may be constitutionally protected." Katz v. United States, 389 U. S. 347, 351-352 (1967). Prior to the digital age, law enforcement might have pursued a suspect for a brief stretch, but doing so "for any extended period of time was difficult and costly and therefore rarely undertaken." *Jones*, 565 U.S. at 429 (opinion of Alito, J.). For that reason, "society's expectation has been that law enforcement agents and others would not—and indeed, in the main, simply could not—secretly monitor and catalogue every

---

[3] The parties suggest as an alternative to their primary submissions that the acquisition of CSLI becomes a search only if it extends beyond a limited period. As part of its argument, the Government treats the seven days of CSLI requested from Sprint as the pertinent period, even though Sprint produced only two days of records. [We] need not decide whether there is a limited period for which the Government may obtain an individual's historical CSLI free from Fourth Amendment scrutiny, and if so, how long that period might be. It is sufficient for our purposes today to hold that accessing seven days of CSLI constitutes a Fourth Amendment search.

single movement of an individual's car for a very long period." *Id.*, at 430. Allowing government access to cell-site records contravenes that expectation. Although such records are generated for commercial purposes, that distinction does not negate Carpenter's anticipation of privacy in his physical location. Mapping a cell phone's location over the course of 127 days provides an all-encompassing record of the holder's whereabouts. As with GPS information, the timestamped data provides an intimate window into a person's life, revealing not only his particular movements, but through them his "familial, political, professional, religious, and sexual associations." *Id.*, at 415 (opinion of Sotomayor, J.). These location records "hold for many Americans the privacies of life." Riley v. California, 134 S. Ct. 2473, 2494 (2014) (quoting Boyd v. United States, 116 U. S. 616, 630 (1886)). And like GPS monitoring, cell phone tracking is remarkably easy, cheap, and efficient compared to traditional investigative tools. With just the click of a button, the Government can access each carrier's deep repository of historical location information at practically no expense.

In fact, historical cell-site records present even greater privacy concerns than the GPS monitoring of a vehicle we considered in *Jones*. Unlike the bugged container in United States v. Knotts, 460 U. S. 276 (1983) or the car in *Jones*, a cell phone—almost a "feature of human anatomy," *Riley*, 134 S. Ct. at 2484—tracks nearly exactly the movements of its owner. While individuals regularly leave their vehicles, they compulsively carry cell phones with them all the time. A cell phone faithfully follows its owner beyond public thoroughfares and into private residences, doctor's offices, political headquarters, and other potentially revealing locales. . . . Accordingly, when the Government tracks the location of a cell phone it achieves near perfect surveillance, as if it had attached an ankle monitor to the phone's user.

Moreover, the retrospective quality of the data here gives police access to a category of information otherwise unknowable. In the past, attempts to reconstruct a person's movements were limited by a dearth of records and the frailties of recollection. With access to CSLI, the Government can now travel back in time to retrace a person's whereabouts, subject only to the retention polices of the wireless carriers, which currently maintain records for up to five years. Critically, because location information is continually logged for all of the 400 million devices in the United States—not just those belonging to persons who might happen to come under investigation—this newfound tracking capacity runs against everyone.

Unlike with the GPS device in *Jones*, police need not even know in advance whether they want to follow a particular individual, or when.

Whoever the suspect turns out to be, he has effectively been tailed every moment of every day for five years, and the police may—in the Government's view—call upon the results of that surveillance without regard to the constraints of the Fourth Amendment. Only the few without cell phones could escape this tireless and absolute surveillance. . . . Accordingly, when the Government accessed CSLI from the wireless carriers, it invaded Carpenter's reasonable expectation of privacy in the whole of his physical movements.

B.

The Government's primary contention to the contrary is that the third-party doctrine governs this case. In its view, cell-site records are fair game because they are "business records" created and maintained by the wireless carriers. The Government . . . recognizes that this case features new technology, but asserts that the legal question nonetheless turns on a garden-variety request for information from a third-party witness. The Government's position fails to contend with the seismic shifts in digital technology that made possible the tracking of not only Carpenter's location but also everyone else's, not for a short period but for years and years. Sprint Corporation and its competitors are not your typical witnesses. Unlike the nosy neighbor who keeps an eye on comings and goings, they are ever alert, and their memory is nearly infallible. There is a world of difference between the limited types of personal information addressed in *Smith* and *Miller* and the exhaustive chronicle of location information casually collected by wireless carriers today. . . .

Neither does the second rationale underlying the third-party doctrine—voluntary exposure—hold up when it comes to CSLI. Cell phone location information is not truly "shared" as one normally understands the term. In the first place, cell phones and the services they provide are such a pervasive and insistent part of daily life that carrying one is indispensable to participation in modern society. Second, a cell phone logs a cell-site record by dint of its operation, without any affirmative act on the part of the user beyond powering up. Virtually any activity on the phone generates CSLI, including incoming calls, texts, or e-mails and countless other data connections that a phone automatically makes when checking for news, weather, or social media updates. Apart from disconnecting the phone from the network, there is no way to avoid leaving behind a trail of location data. As a result, in no meaningful sense does the user voluntarily "assume the risk" of turning over a comprehensive dossier of his physical movements.

We therefore decline to extend *Smith* and *Miller* to the collection of CSLI. Given the unique nature of cell phone location information, the fact that the Government obtained the information from a third party does not overcome Carpenter's claim to Fourth Amendment protection. The Government's acquisition of the cell-site records was a search within the meaning of the Fourth Amendment. . . .

Our decision today is a narrow one. We do not express a view on matters not before us: real-time CSLI or "tower dumps" (a download of information on all the devices that connected to a particular cell site during a particular interval). We do not disturb the application of *Smith* and *Miller* or call into question conventional surveillance techniques and tools, such as security cameras. Nor do we address other business records that might incidentally reveal location information. Further, our opinion does not consider other collection techniques involving foreign affairs or national security. . . .

IV.

Having found that the acquisition of Carpenter's CSLI was a search, we also conclude that the Government must generally obtain a warrant supported by probable cause before acquiring such records. Although the ultimate measure of the constitutionality of a governmental search is "reasonableness," our cases establish that warrantless searches are typically unreasonable where a search is undertaken by law enforcement officials to discover evidence of criminal wrongdoing. . . .

Justice Alito contends that the warrant requirement simply does not apply when the Government acquires records using compulsory process. Unlike an actual search, he says, subpoenas for documents do not involve the direct taking of evidence; they are at most a "constructive search" conducted by the target of the subpoena. . . . But this Court has never held that the Government may subpoena third parties for records in which the suspect has a reasonable expectation of privacy. Almost all of the examples Justice Alito cites contemplated requests for evidence implicating diminished privacy interests or for a corporation's own books. The lone exception, of course, is *Miller*, where the Court's analysis of the third-party subpoena merged with the application of the third-party doctrine. . . .

If the choice to proceed by subpoena provided a categorical limitation on Fourth Amendment protection, no type of record would ever be protected by the warrant requirement. Under Justice Alito's view, private letters, digital contents of a cell phone—any personal information reduced to document form, in fact—may be collected by subpoena for no reason other than "official curiosity." . . .

Further, even though the Government will generally need a warrant to access CSLI, case-specific exceptions may support a warrantless search of an individual's cell-site records under certain circumstances. One well-recognized exception applies when "the exigencies of the situation" make the needs of law enforcement so compelling that a warrantless search is objectively reasonable under the Fourth Amendment. Kentucky v. King, 563 U. S. 452, 460 (2011). Such exigencies include the need to pursue a fleeing suspect, protect individuals who are threatened with imminent harm, or prevent the imminent destruction of evidence.

As a result, if law enforcement is confronted with an urgent situation, such fact-specific threats will likely justify the warrantless collection of CSLI. Lower courts, for instance, have approved warrantless searches related to bomb threats, active shootings, and child abductions. Our decision today does not call into doubt warrantless access to CSLI in such circumstances. While police must get a warrant when collecting CSLI to assist in the mine-run criminal investigation, the rule we set forth does not limit their ability to respond to an ongoing emergency. . . .

As Justice Brandeis explained in his famous dissent, the Court is obligated—as "subtler and more far-reaching means of invading privacy have become available to the Government"—to ensure that the "progress of science" does not erode Fourth Amendment protections. Olmstead v. United States, 277 U. S. 438, 473-474 (1928). Here the progress of science has afforded law enforcement a powerful new tool to carry out its important responsibilities. At the same time, this tool risks Government encroachment of the sort the Framers, after consulting the lessons of history, drafted the Fourth Amendment to prevent. . . .

KENNEDY, J., dissenting.*

. . . The Court has twice held that individuals have no Fourth Amendment interests in business records which are possessed, owned, and controlled by a third party. United States v. Miller, 425 U. S. 435 (1976); Smith v. Maryland, 442 U. S. 735 (1979). This is true even when the records contain personal and sensitive information. So when the Government uses a subpoena to obtain, for example, bank records, telephone records, and credit card statements from the businesses that create and keep these records, the Government does not engage in a search of the business's customers within the meaning of the Fourth Amendment. . . .

Cell-site records . . . are no different from the many other kinds of business records the Government has a lawful right to obtain by compulsory process. Customers like petitioner do not own, possess, control, or use the records, and for that reason have no reasonable expectation that they cannot be disclosed pursuant to lawful compulsory process. . . .

Miller and *Smith* set forth an important and necessary limitation on the *Katz* framework. They rest upon the commonsense principle that the absence of property law analogues can be dispositive of privacy expectations. The defendants in those cases could expect that the third-party businesses could use the records the companies collected, stored, and classified as their own for any number of business and commercial purposes. The businesses were not bailees or custodians of the records, with a duty to hold the records for the defendants' use. The defendants could make no argument that the records were their own papers or effects. . . .

The second principle supporting *Miller* and *Smith* is the longstanding rule that the Government may use compulsory process to compel persons to disclose documents and other evidence within their possession and control. A subpoena is different from a warrant in its force and intrusive power. While a warrant allows the Government to enter and seize and make the examination itself, a subpoena simply requires the person to whom it is directed to make the disclosure. A subpoena, moreover, provides the recipient the opportunity to present objections before complying, which further mitigates the intrusion.

---

* [Justices Thomas and Alito joined this opinion—EDS.]

For those reasons this Court has held that a subpoena for records, although a "constructive" search subject to Fourth Amendment constraints, need not comply with the procedures applicable to warrants—even when challenged by the person to whom the records belong. Rather, a subpoena complies with the Fourth Amendment's reasonableness requirement so long as it is "sufficiently limited in scope, relevant in purpose, and specific in directive so that compliance will not be unreasonably burdensome." Donovan v. Lone Steer, Inc., 464 U. S. 408, 415 (1984). Persons with no meaningful interests in the records sought by a subpoena, like the defendants in *Miller* and *Smith,* have no rights to object to the records' disclosure—much less to assert that the Government must obtain a warrant to compel disclosure of the records. . . .

A person's movements are not particularly private. As the Court recognized in *Knotts*, when the defendant there "traveled over the public streets he voluntarily conveyed to anyone who wanted to look the fact that he was traveling over particular roads in a particular direction, the fact of whatever stops he made, and the fact of his final destination." Today expectations of privacy in one's location are, if anything, even less reasonable than when the Court decided *Knotts* over 30 years ago. Millions of Americans choose to share their location on a daily basis, whether by using a variety of location-based services on their phones, or by sharing their location with friends and the public at large via social media. And cell-site records, as already discussed, disclose a person's location only in a general area. The records at issue here, for example, revealed Carpenter's location within an area covering between around a dozen and several hundred city blocks. . . .

Technological changes involving cell phones have complex effects on crime and law enforcement. Cell phones make crimes easier to coordinate and conceal, while also providing the Government with new investigative tools that may have the potential to upset traditional privacy expectations. See Kerr, An Equilibrium-Adjustment Theory of the Fourth Amendment, 125 Harv. L. Rev 476, 512-517 (2011). How those competing effects balance against each other, and how property norms and expectations of privacy form around new technology, often will be difficult to determine during periods of rapid technological change. In those instances, and where the governing legal standard is one of reasonableness, it is wise to defer to legislative judgments like the one embodied in §2703(d) of the Stored Communications Act. . . .

THOMAS, J., dissenting.

This case should not turn on "whether" a search occurred. It should turn, instead, on *whose* property was searched. The Fourth Amendment guarantees individuals the right to be secure from unreasonable searches of "*their* persons, houses, papers, and effects" (emphasis added). . . . By obtaining the cell-site records of MetroPCS and Sprint, the Government did not search Carpenter's property. He did not create the records, he does not maintain them, he cannot control them, and he cannot destroy them. Neither the terms of his contracts nor any provision of law makes the records his. The records belong to MetroPCS and Sprint.

The Court concludes that, although the records are not Carpenter's, the Government must get a warrant because Carpenter had a reasonable "expectation of privacy" in the location information that they reveal. [This] is not the best reading of our precedents. The more fundamental problem with the Court's opinion, however, is its use of the "reasonable expectation of privacy" test, which was first articulated by Justice Harlan in Katz v. United States, 389 U. S. 347, 360–361 (1967) (concurring opinion). The *Katz* test has no basis in the text or history of the Fourth Amendment. And, it invites courts to make judgments about policy, not law. Until we confront the problems with this test, *Katz* will continue to distort Fourth Amendment jurisprudence. I respectfully dissent. . . .

The *Katz* test strays . . . from the text [of the Fourth Amendment] by focusing on the concept of "privacy." The word "privacy" does not appear in the Fourth Amendment (or anywhere else in the Constitution for that matter). Instead, the Fourth Amendment references the "right of the people to be secure." It then qualifies that right by limiting it to "persons" and three specific types of property: "houses, papers, and effects." By connecting the right to be secure to these four specific objects, the text of the Fourth Amendment reflects its close connection to property. Privacy, by contrast, "was not part of the political vocabulary of the [founding]. Instead, liberty and privacy rights were understood largely in terms of property rights." Cloud, Property Is Privacy: Locke and Brandeis in the Twenty-First Century, 55 Am. Crim. L. Rev. 37, 42 (2018). [The] *Katz* test also has proved unworkable in practice. . . .

Because the *Katz* test is a failed experiment, this Court is dutybound to reconsider it. Until it does, I agree with my dissenting colleagues' reading of our precedents. Accordingly, I respectfully dissent.

ALITO, J. dissenting.*

First, the Court ignores the basic distinction between an actual search (dispatching law enforcement officers to enter private premises and root through private papers and effects) and an order merely requiring a party to look through its own records and produce specified documents. The former, which intrudes on personal privacy far more deeply, requires probable cause; the latter does not. Treating an order to produce like an actual search, as today's decision does, is revolutionary. It violates both the original understanding of the Fourth Amendment and more than a century of Supreme Court precedent. Unless it is somehow restricted to the particular situation in the present case, the Court's move will cause upheaval. Must every grand jury subpoena duces tecum be supported by probable cause? . . .

Second, the Court allows a defendant to object to the search of a third party's property. This also is revolutionary. . . . By departing dramatically from these fundamental principles, the Court destabilizes long-established Fourth Amendment doctrine. We will be making repairs—or picking up the pieces—for a long time to come. . . .

Searches generally begin with officers making nonconsensual entries into areas not open to the public. Once there, officers are necessarily in a position to observe private spaces generally shielded from the public and discernible only with the owner's consent. Private area after private area becomes exposed to the officers' eyes as they rummage through the owner's property in their hunt for the object or objects of the search. If they are searching for documents, officers may additionally have to rifle through many other papers—potentially filled with the most intimate details of a person's thoughts and life—before they find the specific information they are seeking. If anything sufficiently incriminating comes into view, officers seize it. Physical destruction always lurks as an underlying possibility . . . .

Compliance with a subpoena duces tecum requires none of that. A subpoena duces tecum permits a subpoenaed individual to conduct the

---

* [Justice Thomas joined this opinion—EDS.]

search for the relevant documents himself, without law enforcement officers entering his home or rooting through his papers and effects. As a result, subpoenas avoid the many incidental invasions of privacy that necessarily accompany any actual search. . . .

Against centuries of precedent and practice, all that the Court can muster is the observation that "this Court has never held that the Government may subpoena third parties for records in which the suspect has a reasonable expectation of privacy." Frankly, I cannot imagine a concession more damning to the Court's argument than that. As the Court well knows, the reason that we have never seen such a case is because—until today—defendants categorically had no "reasonable expectation of privacy" and no property interest in records belonging to third parties. . . . By implying otherwise, the Court tries the nice trick of seeking shelter under the cover of precedents that it simultaneously perforates. . . .

GORSUCH, J., dissenting.

. . . Can the government demand a copy of all your e-mails from Google or Microsoft without implicating your Fourth Amendment rights? Can it secure your DNA from 23andMe without a warrant or probable cause? *Smith* and *Miller* say yes it can—at least without running afoul of *Katz*. But that result strikes most lawyers and judges today—me included—as pretty unlikely. In the years since its adoption, countless scholars, too, have come to conclude that the "third-party doctrine is not only wrong, but horribly wrong." Kerr, The Case for the Third-Party Doctrine, 107 Mich. L. Rev. 561, 563, n. 5, 564 (2009) (collecting criticisms but defending the doctrine). The reasons are obvious. As an empirical statement about subjective expectations of privacy, the doctrine is "quite dubious." Baude & Stern, The Positive Law Model of the Fourth Amendment, 129 Harv. L. Rev. 1821, 1872 (2016). People often do reasonably expect that information they entrust to third parties, especially information subject to confidentiality agreements, will be kept private. Meanwhile, if the third party doctrine is supposed to represent a normative assessment of when a person should expect privacy, the notion that the answer might be "never" seems a pretty unattractive societal prescription. . . .

What if we dropped *Smith* and *Miller*'s third party doctrine and retreated to the root *Katz* question whether there is a "reasonable expectation of privacy" in data held by third parties? Rather than solve the problem with the third party doctrine, I worry this option only risks returning us to its source: After all, it was *Katz* that produced *Smith* and *Miller* in the first place. *Katz*'s problems start with the text and original understanding of the Fourth Amendment, as Justice Thomas thoughtfully explains today. . . .

Katz has yielded an often unpredictable—and sometimes unbelievable—jurisprudence. . . . Take Florida v. Riley, 488 U. S. 445 (1989), which says that a police helicopter hovering 400 feet above a person's property invades no reasonable expectation of privacy. Try that one out on your neighbors. . . . Or California v. Greenwood, 486 U. S. 35 (1988), which holds that a person has no reasonable expectation of privacy in the garbage he puts out for collection. In that case, the Court said that the homeowners forfeited their privacy interests because it is "common knowledge that plastic garbage bags left on or at the side of a public street are readily accessible to animals, children, scavengers, snoops, and other members of the public." But the habits of raccoons don't prove much about the habits of the country. I doubt, too, that most people spotting a neighbor rummaging through their garbage would think they lacked reasonable grounds to confront the rummager. Resorting to *Katz* in data privacy cases threatens more of the same. . . .

There is another way. From the founding until the 1960s, the right to assert a Fourth Amendment claim didn't depend on your ability to appeal to a judge's personal sensibilities about the "reasonableness" of your expectations or privacy. It was tied to the law. The Fourth Amendment protects "the right of the people to be secure in their persons, houses, papers and effects, against unreasonable searches and seizures." True to those words and their original understanding, the traditional approach asked if a house, paper or effect was yours under law. . . . Under this more traditional approach, Fourth Amendment protections for your papers and effects do not automatically disappear just because you share them with third parties.

Given the prominence *Katz* has claimed in our doctrine, American courts are pretty rusty at applying the traditional approach to the Fourth Amendment. We know that if a house, paper, or effect is yours, you have a Fourth Amendment interest in its protection. But what kind of legal interest is sufficient to make something yours? And what source of law determines that? Current positive law? The common law at 1791, extended by analogy to modern times? Both? . . . Much work is needed to revitalize this area and answer these questions. . . .

First, the fact that a third party has access to or possession of your papers and effects does not necessarily eliminate your interest in them. Ever hand a private document to a friend to be returned? Toss your keys to a valet at a restaurant? Ask your neighbor to look after your dog while you travel? You would not expect the friend to share the document with others; the valet to lend your car to his buddy; or the neighbor to put Fido up for adoption. Entrusting your stuff to others is a bailment. . . . A bailee who uses the item in a different way than he's supposed to, or against the bailor's instructions, is liable for conversion. . . . This approach is quite different from *Smith* and *Miller*'s (counter)-intuitive approach to reasonable expectations of privacy; where those cases extinguish Fourth Amendment interests once records are given to a third party, property law may preserve them. . . .

Second, I doubt that complete ownership or exclusive control of property is always a necessary condition to the assertion of a Fourth Amendment right. Where houses are concerned, for example, individuals can enjoy Fourth Amendment protection without fee simple title. Both the text of the Amendment and the common law rule support that conclusion. People call a house "their" home when legal title is in the bank, when they rent it, and even when they merely occupy it rent free. . . . That is why tenants and resident family members—though they have no legal title—have standing to complain about searches of the houses in which they live. Chapman v. United States, 365 U. S. 610, 616–617 (1961). . . .

Third, positive law may help provide detailed guidance on evolving technologies without resort to judicial intuition. State (or sometimes federal) law often creates rights in both tangible and intangible things. . . .

Fourth, while positive law may help establish a person's Fourth Amendment interest there may be some circumstances where positive law cannot be used to defeat it. Ex parte Jackson, 96 U.S. 727 (1878), reflects that understanding. There this Court said that "no law of Congress" could authorize letter carriers "to invade the secrecy of letters." So the post office couldn't impose a regulation dictating that those mailing letters surrender all legal interests in them once they're deposited in a mailbox. If that is right, *Jackson* suggests the existence of a constitutional floor below which Fourth Amendment rights may not descend.

Fifth, this constitutional floor may, in some instances, bar efforts to circumvent the Fourth Amendment's protection through the use of subpoenas. No one thinks the government can evade *Jackson*'s prohibition on opening sealed letters without a warrant simply by issuing a subpoena to a postmaster for "all letters sent by John Smith" or, worse, "all letters sent by John Smith concerning a particular transaction." So the question courts will confront will be this: What other kinds of records are sufficiently similar to letters in the mail that the same rule should apply? . . .

It seems to me entirely possible a person's cell-site data could qualify as his papers or effects under existing law. Yes, the telephone carrier holds the information. But 47 U. S. C. §222 designates a customer's cell-site location information as "customer proprietary network information" (CPNI) and gives customers certain rights to control use of and access to CPNI about themselves. . . .

The problem is that we do not know anything more. Before the district court and court of appeals, Mr. Carpenter pursued only a *Katz* "reasonable expectations" argument. He did not invoke the law of property or any analogies to the common law, either there or in his petition for certiorari. . . . He offered no analysis . . . of what rights state law might provide him in addition to those supplied by §222. In these circumstances, I cannot help but conclude—reluctantly—that Mr. Carpenter forfeited perhaps his most promising line of argument. . . .

Chapter 8

Interrogations

A. Voluntariness of Confessions

3. Police Lies

Page 527. Add this material at the end of note 5.

Wicklander-Zulawski & Associates, a consulting group that works with many U.S. police departments, announced in 2017 that it would stop training detectives in the "Reid technique" of interrogation, which relies on a claustrophobic room, repeated accusations of guilt, presentation of real or invented evidence, and the slow build-up of pressure. The firm concluded, based on feedback from police departments, that the technique created too many false confessions. See Radley Balko, Big Changes May Be Coming to Police Interrogations, Washington Post, Mar. 10, 2017.

B. Miranda *Warnings*

2. The "Custody" Precondition for *Miranda* Warnings

Page 550. Add this material at the end of note 1.

See also State v. McKenna, 103 A.3d 756 (N.H. 2014) (defendant was in custody and therefore entitled to *Miranda* warnings even though he was in his own yard when police questioned him; defendant was told he was not free to walk away, the questioning was confrontational and accusatory, and the entire episode lasted an hour and 15 minutes).

C. Invocation and Waiver of Miranda *Rights*

Page 575. Add this material at the end of note 3.

See State v. Philpot, 787 S.E.2d 181 (Ga. 2016) (defendant invoked right to counsel when he asked, "You need his number to get him on file?" and followed that with the statement, "You can call [my girlfriend], get her to call him and have him come down here").

F. Miranda *Cures, Impacts, and Alternatives*

3. Alternatives to *Miranda*

Page 624. Add this material at the end of note 3.

See Brandon L. Garrett, Interrogation Policies 49 Univ. Rich. L. Rev. 895 (2015) (study of written police interrogation policies of Virginia law enforcement agencies; over half make recording of interrogation an option, but did not encourage it or provide guidance on how to record; only a handful of policies provided guidance on conducting juvenile interrogations).

Page 626. Add this material at the end of note 1.

See John D. Jackson, Responses to Salduz: Procedural Tradition, Change and the Need for Effective Defence, 79 Modern L. Rev. 987 (2016).

Chapter 9

Identifications

B. Exclusion of Identification Evidence

2. Exclusion on Due Process Grounds

Page 661. Add this material before the Notes.

Commonwealth v. Walter Crayton
21 N.E.3d 157 (Mass. 2014)

GANTS, C.J.

The defendant was convicted by a Superior Court jury on two indictments of possession of child pornography. . . . We granted the defendant's application for direct appellate review. [The defendant] contends that the judge erred in admitting in evidence the in-court identifications of the defendant by two eyewitnesses who had not previously participated in an out-of-court identification procedure. . . . We establish a new standard for the admission of in-court identifications where the eyewitness had not previously participated in an out-of-court identification procedure and conclude that the in-court identifications in this case would not have been admissible under that standard. . . .

Background . . . On January 21, 2009, between approximately 3:30 P.M. and 4:00 P.M., an eighth grade student, M.S., was doing homework at a computer in the basement technology center of the Central Square branch of the Cambridge Public Library. A man she described as short, white, and bald, with a "little beard" and eyeglasses was sitting at an adjacent computer to the right of her. [When asked how long she looked at the person, M.S. answered, "I would say a quick glance."]. She went to the library "mostly every day," but had never seen the man before. When she looked at his computer screen, she saw an image of "a girl about ten years old, covering her chest." She could not tell whether the girl was wearing any clothes, because she saw only a "top view" and the man was "covering the computer screen" with the "umbrella-type" cover that was on it. [M.S. testified that she could see only two or three inches of the computer screen.] She "waved" at her friend, R.M., a ninth grade student, who was also in the technology center of the library, and urged him to look at the man's computer. R.M. testified that he "just got a quick glimpse of the computer," and could only see "a small portion" of the screen, which displayed a young child wearing no clothes. He saw only the side of the man's face; he described the man as bald with a goatee. He went to the library every day after school, but had not seen the man before. During trial, both M.S. and R.M. identified the defendant as the man that they had seen at the computer on January 21.

M.S. and R.M. walked over to Ricardo Negron, a library employee who was working at the staff desk in the technology center that afternoon, and they told him that a person was looking at children wearing no clothes on the computer. Before M.S. and R.M. approached him, Negron had observed M.S. at computer number one and a white male, "perhaps" in his "early thirties," bald, with eyeglasses, whom he had seen before at the technology center, at computer number two. The police later showed Negron an array of photographs, but he was unable to identify anyone from the array.

Library users were required to log on to a computer by entering their library bar code, so when the two teenagers alerted Negron to what they had seen, Negron looked up the log-in information for computer number two. While he was doing so, the man using computer number two logged off and left the room. The log inquiry revealed that a person using the library card of an eighteen year old male, "perhaps of Asian descent," had logged on to computer number two at 3:08 P.M. and logged off at 3:55 P.M. At some time after 3:55 P.M., Negron went upstairs to speak to the library manager, Esme Green. Green went downstairs to the technology center, looked at two "video clips" saved on computer number two, saw that they depicted an approximately twelve year old girl, "either naked or almost naked, masturbating," and telephoned the police.

When Negron went upstairs, another library employee, Ricardo Ricard, went downstairs to staff the technology center. Having learned of the allegation, Ricard logged on to computer number two, saw a folder on the computer with the label "W," and looked at a video file inside the folder, which showed a nude female child. Because he was concerned that the library computers deleted all files when they were shut down for the night, Ricard transferred the folder containing the file to a universal serial bus (USB) drive, which he later gave to Green. He then disabled the computer's "reboot" software so that the computer would retain the files that were then on it.

Ricard had not seen the man who used computer number two on January 21, but he was aware of the man's physical description. On January 22, when he saw a man who matched that description in the library lobby, he told Green of the man's presence, and Green notified the police.

Detectives Brian O'Connor and Pam Clair of the Cambridge police department arrived at the library and saw the defendant at a computer with another individual. The detectives observed the defendant for approximately twenty to thirty minutes at a computer that displayed a "MySpace" profile page, "looking at MySpace." As the defendant was leaving the library, Detective O'Connor asked to speak with him, and the defendant agreed. The defendant admitted that he had been in the library's computer room the previous day. He said he had used one of the computers for five minutes and then switched to another computer, which he identified as computer number two, to check his electronic mail (e-mail). The defendant said that his e-mail address was cblizzard@yahoo.com. He also said that he did not have his own MySpace profile, but used his friend's profile.

After this conversation, Detective O'Connor obtained the USB drive that Ricard had given to Green, seized computer number two, and copied the folder labeled "W" onto a compact disc. After obtaining a search warrant, Detective O'Connor conducted a forensic search of the hard drive of computer number two. That search revealed twenty-seven "cookies," which O'Connor described as "text files" that store information on an Internet browser regarding a Web site that a particular user has visited on the Internet. The first of these cookies, entitled "magic-Lolita(1).txt," was created at 3:14 P.M. on January 21; the last, entitled "www.innocentgirls(1).txt," was created at 3:48 P.M. that day. Detective O'Connor also uncovered "Yahoo searches" on computer number two that had been conducted between 3:14 and 3:25 P.M. on January 21 using such search terms as "One hundred percent Lolita" and "Top Lolita." Detective O'Connor also located temporary Internet files on the computer's hard drive in which images were automatically downloaded by the Internet browser from a Web site that the user visited. In those temporary files, he found approximately 210 photographs where children were engaged in sexual acts, of which seven were printed out and admitted as exhibits at trial. These seven images were created on the computer between 3:27 and 3:50 P.M. on January 21. . . . Detective O'Connor also located a MySpace page in the temporary Internet files reflecting a log-in date and time of January 21 at 3:13 P.M. The MySpace page identifies the user as "Walter"; the e-mail address associated with the MySpace page was C-Blizzard69@MySpace.com. . . .

Discussion . . . Before trial, neither the police nor the prosecutor asked M.S. or R.M. to participate in an identification procedure to determine whether they could identify the man they had seen at the computer on January 21, 2009. They were never shown a photographic array or asked to view a lineup. The first time they were asked to identify the man was on April 7, 2011—more than two years after the first and only time they had seen him—when they were asked by the prosecutor on the witness stand at trial whether they saw the man in the court room, and each identified the defendant.

The defendant moved before trial to preclude the Commonwealth from eliciting an in-court identification of the defendant from any witness that had not previously made an out-of-court identification, including M.S. and R.M. The defendant contended that, under such circumstances, an in-court identification of the defendant would be inherently and unnecessarily suggestive. At a pretrial hearing on the motion, the defendant requested that a voir dire of the teenagers be conducted before any in-court identification was elicited. On the first day of trial, before either M.S. or R.M. had testified, the judge denied the motion, and also denied the request for a voir dire. The judge said that she might reconsider her ruling if the prosecutor failed to lay an adequate foundation through the eyewitnesses' trial testimony before eliciting the in-court identifications. The judge noted that the in-court identifications could not be tainted by a suggestive pretrial identification procedure where there had been none. The judge recognized that "an in-court identification always has some suggestiveness to it," but said that defense counsel could "highlight that suggestiveness" on cross-examination. . . .

We look first to our existing case law on the admission of eyewitness identification testimony. Under art. 12 of the Massachusetts Declaration of Rights, an out-of-court eyewitness identification is not admissible where the defendant proves by a preponderance of the evidence, considering the totality of the circumstances, that the identification is so unnecessarily suggestive and conducive to irreparable misidentification that its admission would deprive the defendant of his right to due process. In contrast with the United States Supreme Court, which has ruled under the Fourteenth Amendment to the United States Constitution that an out-of-court identification that is unnecessarily suggestive will be admissible if it is reliable under "the totality of the circumstances," Manson v. Brathwaite, 432 U.S. 98 (1977), we have said that "the reliability test does little or nothing to discourage police from using suggestive identification procedures," and that only a "rule of per se exclusion can ensure the continued protection against the danger of mistaken identification and wrongful convictions" arising from suggestive identification procedures.

In addition, where an unreliable identification arises from "especially suggestive circumstances" other than an unnecessarily suggestive identification procedure conducted by the police, we have declared that "common law principles of fairness" dictate that the identification should not be admitted. Commonwealth v. Jones, 666 N.E.2d 994 (1996). Our reliance on common-law principles of fairness to suppress an identification made under "especially suggestive circumstances" even where the circumstances did not result from improper police activity is also in contrast with the United States Supreme Court jurisprudence. Compare *id.* with Perry v. New Hampshire, 132 S. Ct. 716 (2012).

We have applied the "unnecessarily suggestive" standard to showup identifications, where the police show a suspect to an eyewitness individually rather than as part of a lineup or photographic array. Such "one-on-one identifications are generally disfavored because they are viewed as inherently suggestive," but suggestiveness alone is not sufficient to render a showup identification inadmissible in evidence; the defendant must prove by a preponderance of the evidence that it was "*unnecessarily* suggestive."

A showup identification may be unnecessarily suggestive for two reasons. First, it may be unnecessarily suggestive where there was not "good reason . . . for the police to use a one-on-one identification procedure." Although "good reason" for a showup identification does not require exigent or special circumstances, there is generally "good reason" where the showup identification occurs within a few hours of the crime, because it is important to learn whether the police have captured the perpetrator or whether the perpetrator is still at large, and because a prompt identification is more likely to be accurate when the witness's recollection of the event is still fresh.

Second, even where there is good reason for a showup identification, it may still be suppressed if the identification procedure "so needlessly adds to the suggestiveness inherent in such an identification that it is conducive to irreparable mistaken identification."[13]

Where, as here, a prosecutor asks a witness at trial whether he or she can identify the perpetrator of the crime in the court room, and the defendant is sitting at counsel's table, the in-court identification is comparable in its suggestiveness to a showup identification. Although the defendant is not alone in the court room, even a witness who had never seen the defendant will infer that the defendant is sitting with counsel at the defense table, and can easily infer who is the defendant

[13] Showups pose an additional risk of misidentification that is not present with lineups or photographic arrays. As the Supreme Judicial Court Study Group on Eyewitness Testimony explained: "Unlike lineups, showups have no mechanism to distinguish witnesses who are guessing from those who actually recognize the suspect. In an unbiased lineup, an unreliable witness will often be exposed by a 'false positive' response identifying a known innocent subject. By contrast, because showups involve a lone suspect, every witness who guesses will positively identify the suspect, and every positive identification is regarded as a 'hit.' For that reason, misidentifications that occur in showups are less likely to be discovered as mistakes." Supreme Judicial Court Study Group on Eyewitness Evidence: Report and Recommendations to the Justices 76 (July 25, 2013). This increased risk of undetected false identification is present in every showup identification, whether conducted out of court or in court.

and who is the attorney.

In fact, in-court identifications may be more suggestive than showups. At a showup that occurs within hours of a crime, the eyewitness likely knows that the police suspect the individual, but unless the police say more than they should, the eyewitness is unlikely to know how confident the police are in their suspicion. However, where the prosecutor asks the eyewitness if the person who committed the crime is in the court room, the eyewitness knows that the defendant has been charged and is being tried for that crime. The presence of the defendant in the court room is likely to be understood by the eyewitness as confirmation that the prosecutor, as a result of the criminal investigation, believes that the defendant is the person whom the eyewitness saw commit the crime. Under such circumstances, eyewitnesses may identify the defendant out of reliance on the prosecutor and in conformity with what is expected of them rather than because their memory is reliable.

Although we have adopted a "rule of per se exclusion" for unnecessarily suggestive out-of-court identifications, we have not adopted such a rule for in-court identifications, despite their comparable suggestiveness. Instead, we have excluded an in-court identification only where it is tainted by an out-of-court confrontation . . . that is "so impermissibly suggestive as to give rise to a very substantial likelihood of irreparable misidentification." In essence, we have excluded in-court identifications only where their inherent suggestiveness is magnified by the impermissible suggestiveness of an out-of-court identification. Therefore, here, where there had been no out-of-court identification to taint the in-court identification, the judge's admission of the in-court identification conformed to our case law. We now do what a trial judge cannot do—revisit the wisdom of our case law regarding the admission of in-court identifications where the eyewitness has not earlier been asked to make an out-of-court identification.

There can be no doubt that, if the police, more than twenty-six months after the incident, had brought M.S. or R.M. to any room other than a court room on the day of trial, identified one of the persons in the room as the defendant, and asked whether the person they had seen looking at images of nude children in the library that day was in the room, we would conclude that the showup identification was unnecessarily suggestive and therefore inadmissible in evidence, especially where this had been the first identification procedure the police had attempted. The question we must confront is whether such an otherwise inadmissible showup identification becomes admissible because the showup occurred in the court room.

A first-time in-court identification differs from an out of court showup in three ways, so we must evaluate whether these differences justify the admission of an in-court identification that would be inadmissible if it occurred out of court. The first difference is that, with an in-court identification, the jury see the identification procedure, whereas the jury do not see a showup identification procedure unless the police videotape the procedure. When a first-time eyewitness identification occurs in court and no suggestive pretrial identification procedures were administered by the state, courts generally have concluded that the factfinder is better able to evaluate the reliability of the identification because he or she can observe the witness's demeanor and hear the witness's statements *during* the identification procedure. [The] jury during an in-court identification [can] see indications of witness certainty or hesitation during the identification process, including facial expression, voice inflection, and body language. . . .

We agree that a jury may be better able to assess a witness's level of confidence during an in-court identification than through evidence of a showup, but we do not agree that this means that a jury are better able to evaluate the accuracy of an in-court identification. Social science research has shown that a witness's level of confidence in an identification is not a reliable predictor of the accuracy of the identification, especially where the level of confidence is inflated by its suggestiveness. See Supreme Judicial Court Study Group on Eyewitness Evidence: Report and Recommendations to the Justices 19 (July 25, 2013).[15] Moreover, even if we were persuaded that there were evaluative

---

[15] Even among "highly confident witnesses, [studies] indicate that 20 to 30% could be in error." Wells, Memon, & Penrod, Eyewitness Evidence: Improving Its Probative Value, 7 Psychol. Sci. in the Pub. Interest 45, 66 (2006). More generally, the less-than-perfect correlation between height and gender in humans is "considerably greater" than the correlation between certainty and accuracy in eyewitness identifications. Wells & Quinlivan, Suggestive Eyewitness Identification Procedures and the Supreme Court's Reliability Test in Light of Eyewitness Science: 30 Years Later, 33 Law & Hum. Behav. 1, 11-12 (2009). Although "psychological scientists have generally concluded that eyewitness certainty . . . can have some diagnostic value" (even if it is of "limited utility"), its diagnostic value is substantially diminished where suggestive identification procedures have been used. Studies have shown, for instance, that "confirmatory

benefits arising from the jury's ability to see the identification procedure, it would not justify admission of an inherently suggestive identification. Certainly, where there was not good reason to conduct an out-of-court showup, an identification arising from such a showup would not be admissible because the police have videotaped it.

The second difference between a first-time in-court identification and a showup is that the former occurs in court, and therefore "is subject to immediate challenge through cross-examination." Some other courts have concluded that "where a witness first identifies the defendant at trial, defense counsel may test the perceptions, memory and bias of the witness, contemporaneously exposing weaknesses and adding perspective in order to lessen the hazards of undue weight or mistake." We are not persuaded that the immediacy of cross-examination materially lessens "the hazards of undue weight or mistake" arising from a suggestive identification. Eyewitnesses are routinely subject to cross-examination regarding their showup identifications, but that does not render such identifications admissible where they are unnecessarily suggestive. Moreover, we have previously recognized how difficult it is for a defense attorney to convince a jury that an eyewitness's confident identification might be attributable to the suggestive influence of the circumstances surrounding the identification. Nor is the immediacy of cross-examination likely to make the cross-examination more effective in revealing the risk of inaccuracy. In fact, such immediacy means that defense counsel has little opportunity to prepare an effective cross-examination regarding the identification, because it occurred minutes earlier.

The third difference between a first-time in-court identification and a showup is that, where defense counsel has advance warning that the prosecutor intends to ask the eyewitness at trial to identify the defendant, defense counsel has the opportunity to propose alternative identification procedures that are less suggestive, such as an in-court line-up, or having the defendant sit somewhere in the courtroom other than the defense table.

We do not join those courts that have placed the burden on the

---

suggestive remarks from the lineup administrator [like 'Good, you identified the actual suspect'] consistently inflate eyewitness certainty for eyewitnesses who are in fact mistaken." . . .

defendant to avoid a suggestive in-court identification by proposing alternative, less suggestive identification procedures. Placing this burden on the defendant suggests that the Commonwealth is entitled to an unnecessarily suggestive in-court identification unless the defendant proposes a less suggestive alternative that the trial judge in his or her discretion adopts. We decline to grant the Commonwealth such an entitlement where, as here, the Commonwealth failed earlier to conduct a less suggestive out-of-court identification procedure, and the in-court identification is therefore the *only* identification of the defendant made by an eyewitness.

Where an eyewitness has not participated before trial in an identification procedure, we shall treat the in-court identification as an in-court showup, and shall admit it in evidence only where there is "good reason" for its admission.[16] The new rule we declare today shall apply prospectively to trials that commence after issuance of this opinion, and shall apply only to in-court identifications of the defendant by eyewitnesses who were present during the commission of the crime.

We recognize that the "good reason" that generally justifies most out-of-court showups—i.e., "concerns for public safety; the need for efficient police investigation in the immediate aftermath of a crime; and the usefulness of prompt confirmation of the accuracy of investigatory information"—depends on the short duration of time between the crime and the showup, and will never justify an in-court showup. But there may be other grounds that constitute "good reason" for an in-court showup where there has not been a nonsuggestive out-of-court identification procedure. For instance, there may be "good reason" for the first identification procedure to be an in-court showup where the eyewitness was familiar with the defendant before the commission of the crime, such as where a victim testifies to a crime of domestic violence. "Good reason" might also exist where the witness is an arresting officer who was also an eyewitness to the commission of the crime, and the identification merely confirms that the defendant is the person who was arrested for the charged crime. In both of these circumstances, the in-

---

[16] We base our decision today on common law principles of fairness. Commonwealth v. Jones, 666 N.E.2d 994 (Mass. 1999) (explaining that common law provides basis for excluding in-court identifications). We do not address whether State constitutional principles would also require "good reason" before in-court identifications are admitted in evidence. Nor do we address the admissibility of in-court identifications in civil cases.

court showup is understood by the jury as confirmation that the defendant sitting in the court room is the person whose conduct is at issue rather than as identification evidence. And in both of these circumstances, where the witness is not identifying the defendant based solely on his or her memory of witnessing the defendant at the time of the crime, there is little risk of misidentification arising from the in-court showup despite its suggestiveness.

Although we generally place the burden on the defendant to move to suppress an identification, that makes little sense where there is no out-of-court identification of the defendant by a witness and only the prosecutor knows whether he or she intends to elicit an in-court identification from the witness. If the burden were on the defendant to move to suppress an identification in these circumstances, a defendant would need to file motions to suppress the in-court identification of witnesses whom the prosecutor might not intend to ask to make such an identification. To avoid the filing of needless motions, we place the burden on the prosecutor to move in limine to admit the in-court identification of the defendant by a witness where there has been no out-of-court identification. Once the motion is filed, the defendant would continue to bear the burden of showing that the in-court identification would be unnecessarily suggestive and that there is not "good reason" for it. Although we impose no restrictions on when such a motion must be filed, a prosecutor would be wise to file it in advance of trial, because, if the defendant were to prevail in suppressing the in-court identification as unnecessarily suggestive, the Commonwealth would still have time, if it chose, to conduct a less suggestive out-of-court identification procedure.

Limiting in-court showups under the "good reason" standard need not diminish the important evidentiary role of reliable eyewitness identifications. Reliable evidence of eyewitness identification will continue to be admissible where it arises from a nonsuggestive out-of-court identification procedure. Where a prosecutor recognizes during trial preparation that no lineup or photographic array has been shown to an eyewitness who may be able to identify the defendant, nothing bars the prosecutor from causing such an identification procedure to be conducted out-of-court before the witness takes the stand. All that is lost by barring first-time in-court showups where there is no "good reason" for such a showup is the unfair evidentiary weight of a needlessly suggestive showup identification that might be given more weight by a jury than it deserves.[20]

In this case, there was no "good reason" for the highly suggestive in-court identifications of M.S. and R.M., where the Commonwealth had abundant opportunity to attempt to obtain a far less suggestive out-of-court identification through a lineup or photographic array. But we cannot conclude that the judge abused her discretion in allowing the in-court identifications in evidence where their admission was in accord with the case law existing at the time of her decision, and where we only today apply the "good reason" standard to first-time in-court showups. [The court then addressed the two further issues related to evidentiary rulings at trial. The court held that the rulings were erroneous, and on that basis vacated the conviction and remanded the case for a new trial.]

Page 663. Add this material after note 5.

6. *Changing In-court identifications*. Massachusetts stakes out new territory on in-court identifications with the *Crayton* decision. Most state and federal courts considering similar issues have come to a different conclusion. See, e.g., Byrd v. State, 25 A.3d 761, 767 (Del. 2011); State v. King, 934 A.2d 556 (N.H. 2007); State v. Lewis, 609 S.E.2d 515 (S.C. 2005). The *Crayton* decision and the decision by other state and federal courts that allow similar in-court identifications all wrestle with broad skepticism about identification evidence in many settings, driven in large part by modern social science research. Such research played a central

[20] The standard we declare regarding the admission of in-court showup identifications differs from the recommendation on in-court identifications offered by the Supreme Judicial Court Study Group on Eyewitness Evidence, which recommended that "in-court identification not be permitted except, in the judge's discretion, on redirect examination, in rebuttal, or in other circumstances where the defendant challenges the witness's ability to make such [an] identification." The report does not explain the reason for this recommendation, or discuss in detail the problems specific to in-court identification. Where there has been no out-of-court identification procedure, the "good reason" standard we establish for in-court showups is more restrictive than the Study Group's recommendation and, we think, more in keeping with the serious concerns raised in the report about the dangers of suggestive eyewitness identification and the difficulty juries have in accurately evaluating the reliability of a suggestive identification. We conclude that the Study Group's recommendation is both overbroad and too narrow. It is overbroad in that it might bar the admission of in-court showups even where identification is not a contested issue at trial. It is too narrow in that it might permit the admission of in-court showups when they are the least reliable: when the defendant has plausibly challenged the ability of an eyewitness to make a reliable identification of the defendant. . . .

role in *Crayton*, and in the Massachusetts study on which the Court heavily relied. Social scientists have raised concerns about identification evidence for decades. Are there better mechanisms than common law or constitutional adjudication by courts to integrate the knowledge of social scientists into the law?

Page 667. Add this material at the end of note 1.

See Commonwealth v. Thomas, 68 N.E.3d 1161 (Mass. 2017) (police failure to follow department protocol by displaying photos simultaneously did not warrant suppression of identification).

C. *Other Remedies for Improper Identification Procedures*

Page 675. Add this material at the end of note 1.

See also Commonwealth v. Gomes, 22 N.E.3d 897 (Mass. 2015) (social science research establishes five principles of eyewitness identification that must be reflected in jury instructions regardless of whether the accused presented expert testimony on them); Nell Greenfield-Boyce, A Judge's Guidance Makes Jurors Suspicious of Any Eyewitness, National Public Radio, Jan. 26, 2016, available at http://www.npr.org/sections/health-shots/2016/01/26/464300484/a-judges-guidance-makes-jurors-suspicious-of-any-eyewitness.

Page 677. Add this material at the end of note 5.

See also Kathy Pezdek, A Preliminary Study of How Plea Bargaining Decisions by Prosecution and Defense Attorneys Are Affected by Eyewitness Factors (March 2012, NCJ 238136), available at https://www.ncjrs.gov/pdffiles1/nij/grants/238136.pdf.

Chapter 11

Defense Counsel

A. When Will Counsel Be Provided?

1. Types of Charges

Page 749. Add this material at the end of note 1.

In McWilliams v. Dunn, 137 S. Ct. 1790 (2017), the Supreme Court stressed that a simple examination of the defendant by a psychological does not fulfill the *Ake* requirements. An indigent defendant who meets the preconditions must have "access to a competent psychiatrist who will conduct an appropriate [1] examination and assist in [2] evaluation, [3] preparation, and [4] presentation of the defense." In this case, a volunteer psychologist examined the defendant and offered an opinion prior to trial, but no expert was available to defense counsel to review new psychological findings and documents in preparation for the sentencing.

2. Type of Proceedings

Page 758. Add this material at the end of note 3.

See also Report of The Constitution Project National Right to Counsel Committee, "Pretrial Justice and the Right to Counsel at First Judicial Bail Hearing" (May 2015), at http://bit.ly/1LeWoC1.

Page 759. Add this material at the end of note 7.

See Davila v. Davis, 137 S. Ct. 2058 (2017) (defendant cannot not obtain federal habeas corpus relief based on a substantial but procedurally defaulted claim of ineffective assistance of state postconviction counsel).

B. Selection and Rejection of Counsel

Page 767. Add this material at the end of note 2.

See also Commonwealth v. Brooks, 104 A.3d 466 (Pa. 2014) (no abuse of discretion when trial judge turned down a defendant's last-minute request for a continuance to make arrangements to represent himself).

Page 769. Add this material at the end of note 8.

See also Luis v. United States, 578 U.S. __ (2016) pretrial freeze of a criminal defendant's legitimate, untainted assets for potential forfeiture violates the Sixth Amendment right to counsel of choice.

C. Adequacy of Counsel

Page 786. Add this material at the end of note 4.

See also Maryland v. Kulbicki, 136 S. Ct. 2 (2015) (appellate court may not assess trial counsel's performance post hoc based on scientific advances not available at the time of trial).

Page 786. Add this material at the end of note 5.

Weaver v. Massachusetts, 137 S. Ct. 1899 (2017) (claimant who objects to attorney's failure to object to closure of courtroom to public, which amounts to structural error for purposes of harmless error analysis on appeal, must nonetheless prove prejudice for purposes of ineffective assistance claim); Woods v. Donald, 135 S. Ct. 1372 (2015) (state court held that attorney did not provide per se ineffective assistance of counsel when he was absent from trial for ten minutes during testimony concerning other defendants; this conclusion was not an unreasonable application of *Cronic*).

Page 791. Add this material after note 5.

6. *Loss of license*. In extreme cases of inadequate representation, attorneys can lose their license to practice law, based on a breach of the duty of competence. See In re Hawver, 339 P.3d 573 (Kan. 2014) (attorney disbarred for inadequate performance in capital murder case; he accepted case without adequate experience in such litigation and adopted client's preferred defense, claiming that he was innocent because he was a street-smart criminal who would never have left an eyewitness alive to identify him, as the perpetrator did in this case).

D. Systems for Providing Counsel

Page 805. Add this material at the end of note 4.

See also Jed Lipinski, The Trials and Travails of a New Orleans Public Defender, New Orleans Times-Picayune, Mar. 30, 2016, available at http://www.nola.com/crime/index.ssf/2016/03/new_orleans_public_defender_trials_and_travails.html; Debra Cassens Weiss, Louisiana's Public Defender Service is Understaffed by About 1400 Lawyers, ABA Study Finds, ABA Journal, Feb. 17, 2017 (caseload study concludes that 1,769 full-time public defenders are needed to provide reasonably effective assistance of counsel in Louisiana, but the state only employs 363 full-time equivalent PDs).

Page 806. Add this material at the end of note 6.

See also Pamela Metzger and Andrew Guthrie Ferguson, Defending Data, 88 S. Cal. L. Rev. 101 (2015) (proposing collection and use of performance metrics by managers of public defender offices).

E. The Ethics of Defending Criminals

Page 823. Add this material at the end of note 3.

See Garrett Epps, The Nobility of Good Lawyers with Bad Clients, The Atlantic, Feb 7, 2016, available at http://www.theatlantic.com/politics/archive/2016/02/the-nobility-of-good-lawyers-with-bad-clients/459645/.

Chapter 12

Pretrial Release and Detention

A. *Pretrial Release*

1. Change in Bail Practices

Page 837. Add this material at the end of note 4.

Several state and local governments are actively debating methods of restricting the use of money bail and the role of bond dealers. Maryland provides one prominent example. The state Attorney General issued an opinion in October 2016 noting a potential constitutional problem with a release system that keeps poor defendants in jail longer because they cannot afford bail. The Maryland Court of Appeals responded with a revision of procedure rules that disfavored money bail as a condition of release. The bail bond industry tried, without success, to convince the state legislature to pass a statute rolling back the new rule and preserving the role of bond dealers in pretrial release. See Michael Dresser, Busch: Maryland House Will Not Vote on Cash Bail Bill, Baltimore Sun, April 6, 2017.

Equally big changes are under discussion in Texas. A federal judge in Houston issued a preliminary injunction in April 2017 in a civil rights suit filed by a woman arrested for driving with an invalid license and remained in jail for two days because she could not afford bail. The judge ordered Harris County to restrict its use of money bail. Eli Rosenberg, Judge in Houston Strikes Down Harris County's Bail System, N.Y. Times, April 29, 2017. Meanwhile, Harris County officials debated various changes to local practice and the Texas state legislature considered a comprehensive overhaul of the pretrial release system.

Changes to bail practices are also underway in New York. In 2015, New York City adopted a plan to reduce the number of defendants held on bail. About 14 percent of criminal defendants in New York City at that time were held on bail, while 41 percent were released on their own recognizance. The new plan allows judges to replace bail for low-risk defendants with supervision options including daily check-ins, text-message reminders and required drug or behavioral therapy. Judges rely on a risk-assessment tool to gauge a person's threat to public safety and eligibility for release.

Bail practices became a topic of public concern after a series of press reports about defendants held on minor charges for long periods under harsh conditions in the Rikers Island jail. For instance, the Associated Press reported on the case of a mentally ill homeless man who was unable to make $2,500 bail for trespassing and died in Rikers. Another case involved Kalief Browder, who was unable to make $3,000 bail on charges that he stole a backpack at age 16. He was held in Rikers for three years, beaten by inmates and guards alike and held in solitary confinement before charges against him were eventually dropped.

Page 837. Insert the following material at the end of note 5.

In several large urban jurisdictions, the potential savings in jail operation costs have figured prominently in efforts to restrict the use of money bail. For instance, New Mexico voters in 2016 approved an amendment to the state constitution allowing greater pretrial release options for non-dangerous defendants.

The costs of operating a crowded jail also figure into the recommendations of some prosecutors at bail hearings. For instance, the state attorney for Cook County, Illinois (Chicago) announced in 2017 that prosecutors will recommend the release of some defendants charged with minor offenses. The policy statement from the office cited the unjust outcome of detaining defendants based on their wealth and the need to earn community trust. The public debate, however, also referred at times to the costs for taxpayers. See Megan Crepeau, Bail Reform in Cook County Gains Momentum, Chicago Tribune, June 12, 2017.

2. Who Sets Bail?

Page 843. Insert the following material at the end of note 4.

Some pretrial release systems also operate on the basis of input from the larger community. In a few places, local civic and religious groups create "community bail funds" that post bail for individuals who cannot assemble the necessary funds from personal or family funds. They do so based on the belief that the courts rely too heavily on bail to ensure public safety and to prevent flight. See Jocelyn Simonson, Bail Nullification, 115 Mich. L. Rev. 585 (2017).

B. Pretrial Detention

Page 856. Add this material at the end of note 1.

It is also possible for a defendant to file a civil suit for damages under 42 U.S.C. § 1983 based on a Fourth Amendment violation if a city detains the defendant improperly after the probable cause to support an arrest no longer exists. In Manuel v. City of Joliet, Illinois, 137 S. Ct. 911 (2017), police arrested a suspect on drug charges but the police laboratory determined that the pills found on the defendant contained no controlled substances. The city, however, detained Manuel for 48 days. The Supreme Court held that Manuel could challenge his pretrial detention on Fourth Amendment grounds.

Page 858. Add this material at the end of note 7.

Shima Baradaran Baughman, Costs of Pretrial Detention, 97 Boston Univ. L. Rev. 1 (2017); Samuel Wiseman, Fixing Bail, 84 Geo. Wash. L. Rev. 417 (2016); Megan Stevenson, Distortion of Justice: How the Inability to Pay Bail Affects Case Outcomes (Univ. Pennsylvania Working Paper, 2016) available at https://ssrn.com/abstract=2777615.

Chapter 13

Charging

A. *Police Screening*

Page 870. Insert the following material at the end of note 2.

See Natasha Lindstrom, Allegheny County DA Zappala Wants Police to Seek Prosecutor's Approval on Felony Charges, Pittsburgh Tribune-Review, Feb. 9, 2017, available at http://triblive.com/local/allegheny/11920646-74/zappala-county-office.

B. *Prosecutorial Screening*

1. Encouraging or Mandating Criminal Charges

Page 878. Insert the following material before the Notes.

In re Affidavits Relating to Timothy Loehmann and Frank Garmback

Cleveland Municipal Court (June 11, 2015)

ADRINE, J.

On June 9, 2015, [eight people] jointly and severally filed with the Cleveland Municipal Court affidavits accusing Cleveland Police Patrol

Officers Timothy Loehmann and Frank Garmback with crimes arising from the shooting death of 12 year-old Tamir Rice on November 22, 2014, within the City of Cleveland. Each of the affiants alleged, in separate parts of their respective affidavits, that each of the accused, by their actions, committed the following violations of the law during the events that resulted in Tamir's death:

1. Aggravated Murder
2. Murder
3. Involuntary Manslaughter
4. Reckless Homicide
5. Negligent Homicide
6. Dereliction of Duty

Generally, the initiation of criminal proceedings in the State of Ohio is the preserve of the prosecuting attorney within a given jurisdiction. However, state law does provide an avenue for a private citizen having knowledge of facts to initiate the criminal process. R.C. 2935.09 provides private citizens the ability to bring forward accusations by affidavit to cause an arrest or prosecution. As relevant to the situation now before this bench, that section reads in pertinent part:

> (A) As used in this section, "reviewing official" means a judge of the court of record, the prosecuting attorney or attorney charged by law with the prosecution of offenses in a court or before a magistrate, or a magistrate.. . .
> (D) A private citizen having knowledge of the facts who seeks to cause an arrest or prosecution under this section may file an affidavit charging the offense committed with a reviewing official for the purpose of review to determine *if* a complaint should be filed by the *prosecuting attorney or attorney charged by law with the prosecution of offenses* in the court or before the magistrate. . . ."

In each of the affidavits filed with the court in this matter, the affiants related that they had the opportunity to view the surveillance video taken at the time of the complained of event. . . . The video in question in this case is notorious and hard to watch. After viewing it several times, this court is still thunderstruck by how quickly this event turned deadly. The relevant portion covers 18 seconds immediately preceding the point where Tamir Rice suffers the wound, doubles-up and falls to the ground. On the video, the Zone Car containing Patrol Officers Loehmann and Garmback is still in the process of stopping when Rice is shot.

Following the shooting, four additional minutes pass, during which neither officer approaches Tamir as he lies wounded on the ground. At close to four minutes, a young lady, who news reports have since identified as Tamir's sister arrives on the scene and is restrained from going to her brother's side. Nearly eight minutes go by before paramedics arrive at the location. During that same time, approximately six other members of the Cleveland Division of Police join the first two and appear on the video. It is difficult to discern, because of the quality of the tape, what, if any, first aid anyone renders to Rice during these eight minutes. Nearly fourteen minutes ultimately expire between the time that Tamir is shot and the time that he is removed from the park.

The video depicts Rice approaching the Zone Car just as it pulls into the part but it does not appear to show him making any furtive movement prior to, or at, the moment he is shot. Again, because of the quality of the video, the young man's arms are barely visible, but they do not appear to be raised or out-stretched. In the moments immediately before, and as the Zone Car approaches, the video does not display the toy gun in Tamir's hands. There appears to be little if any time reflected on the video for Rice to react or respond to any verbal or audible commands given from Loehmann and Garmback from their Zone Car between the time that they first arrived and the time that Rice was short. Literally, the entire encounter is over in an instant.

Beyond the videos presented as exhibits, each affidavit sets forth the statutory language of each offense alleged.. . . None of the affidavits in this matter provide any other factual basis to justify their requests for the issue of the respective complaints. In order for this court to be in the position to adequately assess the validity of the accusations found therein, those affidavits must be reviewed to determine if, at minimum, the three requirements essential for issuance of a criminal complaint: (1) they must set forth a written statement of facts that constitute the essential elements of the offense charged. The essential elements of a given offense are those facts that must be proven to obtain a conviction, (2) they must state the numerical designations of the Revised Code Sections allegedly violated, and (3) they must be made under oath before a person authorized to administer oaths. Upon completion of this review, the court finds that each of the documents before it meets these minimum requirements.

According to the statute, once the reviewing official is presented the affidavits called for by R.C. 2935.09, the official is required to make a determination as to the appropriate actions needed to substantiate or debunk the allegations contained in each document.

At the beginning of this review, this court is mindful that despite any conclusions it draws from the evidence found in the affidavits, its role here is advisory in nature. The actual issuance of misdemeanor complaints by the City of Cleveland, following the court's review, may be based upon the court's determination that such charges should issue. The decision is completely within the discretion of the City's prosecuting authority.

The City Prosecutor may also decide to issue felony complaints in the Cleveland Municipal Court based upon his acceptance of the court's determination that there is probable cause to believe certain accusations found in the affidavits posted against these Patrol Officers. However, those felony charges and perhaps some, or all, of the misdemeanor charges must ultimately be delivered to the Cuyahoga County Prosecuting Attorney and, will then be subject to *his* discretion, and resolved in the Cuyahoga County Court of Common Pleas.

Resort to this statutory process does not provide an "end around" either the City of the County Prosecutor. The statute provides this court the ability to review affidavits filed by private citizens for sufficiency and good faith. It utilizes the standard of probable cause, the lowest standard of proof required in any criminal proceeding for the conduct of that review. That statutory schema does not, however, provide the court the ability to require that its determination be substituted for the discretion of either the City or the County Prosecuting authorities. . . .

In point of fact, close examination of the applicable statutes and criminal rules reveals that the trial court does not have the option of unilaterally issuing a warrant on its own initiative in these private citizen initiated cases. R.C. 2935.09 provides for the initiation of a criminal action by a "peace officer" or "private citizen." The statute was revised in 2006. . . .

Under the prior version of the statue, there were two ways that a prosecution could be initiated by a private citizen; the first method was by the filing of an affidavit with a judge or clerk of the court of record, and the second was by filing an affidavit with the prosecuting attorney who, in turn, would file a complaint. . . .

Under the amended statute, the ability of a private citizen to "cause prosecution" by filing an affidavit is now limited. . . . Under the current version of the statute . . . a private citizen, to "cause prosecution," now must file an affidavit with a "reviewing official" for *the purpose of review* to determine *if* a complaint should be filed *by the prosecutor*.

[This] court determines that complaints should be filed by the Prosecutor of the City of Cleveland and/or the Cuyahoga County Prosecutor, in re: the accusations levied . . . against the accused, Frank Garmback, in re: Negligent Homicide and Dereliction of Duty.

[This] court . . . determines that complaints should be filed . . . in re: the accusations levied . . . against the accused Timothy Loehmann, for Murder, Involuntary Manslaughter, Reckless Homicide, Negligent Homicide and Dereliction of Duty. . . .

To reach these determinations, this court applies the standard of probable cause, i.e., more than a mere suspicion but less than the quantum of evidence required for conviction. The prosecutors, however, are ethically required to decide whether, applying the highest standard of proof required by law, to wit: beyond a reasonable doubt, it is more likely than not that a reasonable trier of fact will hold the individuals accused in these affidavits accountable for these, or any other crimes that might be alleged. . . .

2. Declination and Diversion

Page 890. Insert the following material at the end of note 4.

In the New York County (Manhattan) District Attorney's office, Cyrus Vance has announced a series of policies that result in declinations for several types of high-volume minor offenses, such as turnstile jumping. See James C. McKinley, Jr., For Manhattan Fare Beaters, One-Way Ticket to Court May be Over, N.Y. Times, June 30, 2017; Emily Ngo, Cyrus Vance to Stop Prosecuting Some Low-Level Manhattan Offenses, Newsday, Mar. 1, 2016.

4. Selection of Charges and System

Page 919. Insert the following material after Problem 13-4.

Department Charging and Sentencing Policy

U.S. Department of Justice
Attorney General of the United States
May 10, 2017

This memorandum establishes charging and sentencing policy for the Department of Justice. Our responsibility is to fulfill our role in a way that accords with the law, advances public safety, and promotes respect for our legal system. It is of the utmost importance to enforce the law fairly and consistently. Charging and sentencing recommendations are crucial responsibilities for any federal prosecutor. The directives I am setting forth below are simple but important. They place great confidence in our prosecutors and supervisors to apply them in a thoughtful and disciplined manner, with the goal of achieving just and consistent results in federal cases.

First, it is a core principle that prosecutors should charge and pursue the most serious, readily provable offense. This policy affirms our responsibility to enforce the law, is moral and just, and produces consistency. This policy fully utilizes the tools Congress has given us. By definition, the most serious offenses are those that carry the most substantial guidelines sentence, including mandatory minimum sentences.

There will be circumstances in which good judgment would lead a prosecutor to conclude that a strict application of the above charging policy is not warranted. In that case, prosecutors should carefully consider whether an exception may be justified. Consistent with longstanding Department of Justice policy, any decision to vary from the policy must be approved by a United States Attorney or Assistant Attorney General, or a supervisor designated by the United States Attorney or Assistant Attorney General, and the reasons must be documented in the file.

Second, prosecutors must disclose to the sentencing court all facts that impact the sentencing guidelines or mandatory minimum sentences, and should in all cases seek a reasonable sentence under the factors in 18

U.S.C. § 3553. In most cases, recommending a sentence within the advisory guideline range will be appropriate. Recommendations for sentencing departures or variances require supervisory approval, and the reasoning must be documented in the file.

Any inconsistent previous policy of the Department of Justice relating to these matters is rescinded, effective today. Each United States Attorney and Assistant Attorney General is responsible for ensuring that this policy is followed, and that any deviations from the core principle are justified by unusual facts. I have directed the Deputy Attorney General to oversee implementation of this policy and to issue any clarification and guidance he deems appropriate for its just and consistent application.

Working with integrity and professionalism, attorneys who implement this policy will meet the high standards required of the Department of Justice for charging and sentencing.

Chapter 14

Jeopardy and Joinder

A. Double Jeopardy

2. "Same Offence"

Page 976. Insert the following material at the end of note 2.

State v. Silvas, 343 P.3d 616 (N.M. 2015) (prosecutors violated defendant's double jeopardy rights by putting him on trial for both drug trafficking and conspiring to engage in drug trafficking on the basis of a single drug transaction; although the statutes contain different elements "in the abstract," the state's theory of the case and the jury instructions reveals that both charges rested upon the single act of transferring the drugs from the defendant's hand to the buyer's hand. Conspiracy can be based on the substantive offense and not violate double jeopardy when it involves "multilayered conduct in which evidence of the conspiracy did not rely solely on evidence of the substantive crime"); United States v. Luong, 393 F.3d 913 (9th Cir. 2004) (allowing successive prosecutions for RICO and predicate offenses, even when predicate offense is conspiracy).

Page 976. Insert the following material at the end of note 3.

People v. Miller, 869 N.W.2d 204 (Mich. 2015) (convicting a man of both drunken driving and drunken driving that caused serious injury to another person violated the double jeopardy clauses of the U.S. Constitution and the Michigan Constitution; statutes do not explicitly authorize multiple punishments).

3. Collateral Estoppel

Page 985. Insert the following material at the end of note 1.

In Bravo-Fernandez v. United States, 137 S. Ct. 352 (2016), a unanimous Court answered a very narrow question, and held that when a jury issues inconsistent verdicts, and where the guilty verdicts are vacated on appeal, ultimate issues of fact may again be litigated in a future lawsuit—in other words, while the acquittal precludes prosecution for the same offense, issue preclusion does not attach. In this case a jury convicted defendants of the federal bribery statute (18 U.S.C. § 666), and simultaneously acquitted them of conspiracy to violate the same statute. Since the additional elements of conspiracy were uncontested, the verdicts were inconsistent. The Court explained that issue preclusion does not apply when verdict inconsistency renders unanswerable "what the jury necessarily decided." See also Currier v. Virginia, 2018 WL 3073763 (June 22, 2018) (because defendant consented to a severance of the multiple charges against him, his second trial and resulting conviction, following an acquittal at his first trial, did not violate the double jeopardy clause).

Chapter 15

Discovery and Speedy Trial

A. Discovery

1. Prosecution Disclosure of Inculpatory Information

Page 1015. Insert the following material at the end of note 3.

See also Jenia I. Turner, Allison D. Redlich, Two Models of Pre-Plea Discovery in Criminal Cases: An Empirical Comparison, 73 Washington & Lee Law Review 285 (2016) (survey of attorneys in North Carolina and Virginia, comparing practices under broad and narrow discovery rules).

Page 1017. Insert the following material at the end of note 8.

See also In re A.B., 99 A.3d 782 (N.J. 2014) (defense counsel is entitled to inspect a crime scene in a victim's home when counsel is able to articulate "a reasonable basis to believe the inspection will lead to relevant evidence on a material issue" and the trial judge makes the inspection "subject to appropriate time, place, and manner restrictions").

2. Prosecution Disclosure of Exculpatory Information

Page 1027. Insert the following material at the end of note 1.

See also Wearry v. Cain, 136 S. Ct. 1002 (2016) (State's failure to disclose material evidence including inmates' statements casting doubt on credibility of State's star witness violated defendant's due process rights).

Page 1028. Insert the following material at the end of note 4.

In Turner v. United States, 137 S. Ct. 1885 (2017), the court affirmed a murder conviction and held that clearly exculpatory evidence was not material to guilt or punishment. The prosecution's theory and evidence at trial was that a large group (including the seven convicted defendants) had committed the murder. The government's evidence included confessions from two of the participants. The undisclosed evidence included identification and impeachment evidence that the defense claimed should cast doubt on the theory of a group murder. The majority lined up the government's evidence and the *Brady* materials and concluded it was "too little, too weak, or too distant from the main evidentiary points to meet *Brady*'s standards." The majority emphasized how much of the government's evidence a jury would need to disbelieve, including both participant confessions and evidence from disinterested witnesses, for the *Brady* material to lead to a different outcome.

Page 1029. Insert the following material at the end of note 5.

See also Miriam Baer, Timing *Brady*, 115 Colum. L. Rev. 1 (2015).

Page 1037. Insert the following material at the end of note 2.

In October 2014, the ABA issued a new Formal Opinion 467, called "Managerial and Supervisory Obligations of Prosecutors under Rules 5.1 and 5.3." This Opinion discusses the ethical obligations of supervisory prosecutors to create a "culture of compliance" with regard to discovery. It explores the use of office-wide policies and training on discovery, including ethical obligations.

B. Speedy Trial Preparation

3. Statutory Protections for Speedy Trial After Accusation

Page 1080. Insert the following material at the end of note 2.

See also Shon Hopwood, The Not So Speedy Trial Act, 89 Wash. L. Rev. 709 (2014).

Page 1081. Insert the following material at the end of note 4.

See also Commonwealth v. Taylor, 14 N.E.3d 955 (Mass. 2014) (defense demands that the prosecution comply with its statutory obligation to turn over certain material without being asked tolls the speedy trial clock, unlike other discovery requests).

Chapter 16

Pleas and Bargains

A. *Bargain About What?*

Page 1092. Place this material after Problem 16-1.

Department Policy on Waiver of Claims of Ineffective Assistance of Counsel

U.S. Department of Justice
James M. Cole, Deputy Attorney General
October 14, 2014

As we all recognize, the right to effective assistance of counsel is a core value of our Constitution. The Department of Justice has a strong interest in ensuring that individuals facing criminal charges receive effective assistance of counsel so that our adversarial system can function fairly, efficiently, and responsibly. Accordingly, in recent years, the Department has made support of indigent defense a priority. We have worked to ensure that all jurisdictions—federal, state, and local—fulfill their obligations under the Constitution to provide effective assistance of counsel, especially to those who cannot afford an attorney.

When negotiating a plea agreement, the majority of United States Attorney's offices do not seek a waiver of claims of ineffective assistance of counsel. This is true even though the federal courts have uniformly held a defendant may generally waive ineffective assistance claims pertaining to matters other than entry of the plea itself, such as claims related to sentencing. While the Department is confident that a waiver of a claim of ineffective assistance of counsel is both legal and ethical, in order to bring consistency to this practice, and in support of the underlying Sixth Amendment right, we now set forth uniform Department of Justice policies relating to waivers of claims of ineffective assistance of counsel.

Federal prosecutors should no longer seek in plea agreements to have a defendant waive claims of ineffective assistance of counsel whether those claims are made on collateral attack or, when permitted by circuit law, made on direct appeal. For cases in which a defendant's ineffective assistance claim would be barred by a previously executed waiver, prosecutors should decline to enforce the waiver when defense counsel rendered ineffective assistance resulting in prejudice or when the defendant's ineffective assistance claim raises a serious debatable issue that a court should resolve.

As long as prosecutors exempt ineffective assistance claims from their waiver provisions, they are free to request waiver of appeal and of post-conviction remedies to the full extent permitted by law as a component of plea discussions and agreements.

Jae Lee v. United States
137 S. Ct. 1958 (2017)

ROBERTS, C.J.*

Petitioner Jae Lee was indicted on one count of possessing ecstasy with intent to distribute. Although he has lived in this country for most of his life, Lee is not a United States citizen, and he feared that a criminal conviction might affect his status as a lawful permanent resident. His attorney assured him there was nothing to worry about—the Government would not deport him if he pleaded guilty. So Lee, who had no real defense to the charge, opted to accept a plea that carried a lesser prison sentence than he would have faced at trial.

Lee's attorney was wrong: The conviction meant that Lee was subject to mandatory deportation from this country. Lee seeks to vacate his conviction on the ground that, in accepting the plea, he received ineffective assistance of counsel in violation of the Sixth Amendment. Everyone agrees that Lee received objectively unreasonable representation. The question presented is whether he can show he was prejudiced as a result.

I.

Jae Lee moved to the United States from South Korea in 1982. He was 13 at the time. His parents settled the family in New York City, where they opened a small coffee shop. After graduating from a business high school in Manhattan, Lee set out on his own to Memphis, Tennessee, where he started working at a restaurant. After three years, Lee decided to try his hand at running a business. With some assistance from his family, Lee opened the Mandarin Palace Chinese Restaurant in a Memphis suburb. The Mandarin was a success, and Lee eventually opened a second restaurant nearby. In the 35 years he has spent in the country, Lee has never returned to South Korea. He did not become a United States citizen, living instead as a lawful permanent resident.

At the same time he was running his lawful businesses, Lee also engaged in some illegitimate activity. In 2008, a confidential informant told federal officials that Lee had sold the informant approximately 200 ecstasy pills and two ounces of hydroponic marijuana over the course of eight years. The officials obtained a search warrant for Lee's house, where they found 88 ecstasy pills, three Valium tablets, $32,432 in cash, and a loaded rifle. Lee admitted that the drugs were his and that he had given ecstasy to his friends.

A grand jury indicted Lee on one count of possessing ecstasy with intent to distribute in violation of 21 U.S.C. § 841(a)(1). Lee retained an attorney and entered into plea discussions with the Government. The attorney advised Lee that going to trial was "very risky" and that, if he pleaded guilty, he would receive a lighter sentence than he would if convicted at trial. Lee informed his attorney of his noncitizen status and repeatedly asked him whether he would face deportation as a result of the criminal proceedings. The attorney told Lee that he would not be deported as a result of pleading guilty. Based on that assurance, Lee accepted the plea and the District Court sentenced him to a year and a day in prison, though it deferred commencement of Lee's sentence for two months so that Lee could manage his restaurants over the holiday season.

Lee quickly learned, however, that a prison term was not the only consequence of his plea. Lee had pleaded guilty to what qualifies as an "aggravated felony" under the Immigration and Nationality Act, and a noncitizen convicted of such an offense is subject to mandatory deportation. Upon learning that he would be deported after serving his sentence, Lee filed a motion under 28 U.S.C. § 2255 to vacate his conviction and sentence, arguing that his attorney had provided constitutionally ineffective assistance.

At an evidentiary hearing on Lee's motion, both Lee and his plea-stage counsel testified that "deportation was the determinative issue in Lee's decision whether to accept the plea." In fact, Lee explained, his attorney became "pretty upset because every time something comes up I always ask about immigration status," and the lawyer "always said why [are you] worrying about something that you don't need to worry about." According to Lee, the lawyer assured him that if deportation was not in the plea agreement, "the government cannot deport you." Lee's attorney testified that he thought Lee's case was a "bad case to try" because Lee's defense to the charge was weak. The attorney nonetheless acknowledged that if he had known Lee would be deported upon pleading guilty, he would have advised him to go to trial. Based on the hearing testimony, a Magistrate Judge recommended that Lee's plea be set aside and his conviction vacated because he had received ineffective assistance of counsel.

The District Court, however, denied relief. Applying our two-part test for ineffective assistance claims from Strickland v. Washington, 466 U.S. 668 (1984), the District Court concluded that . . . "would have almost certainly" been found guilty and received "a significantly longer prison sentence, and subsequent deportation," had he gone to trial. Lee therefore could not show he was prejudiced by his attorney's erroneous advice. . . .

II.

The Sixth Amendment guarantees a defendant the effective assistance of counsel at "critical stages of a criminal proceeding," including when he enters a guilty plea. Lafler v. Cooper, 566 U.S. 156 (2012). To demonstrate that counsel was constitutionally ineffective, a defendant must show that counsel's representation fell below an objective standard of reasonableness and that he was prejudiced as a result. The first requirement is not at issue in today's case: The Government concedes that Lee's plea-stage counsel provided inadequate representation when he assured Lee that he would not be deported if he pleaded guilty. The question is whether Lee can show he was prejudiced by that erroneous advice.

A.

. . . When a defendant alleges his counsel's deficient performance led him to accept a guilty plea rather than go to trial, we do not ask whether, had he gone to trial, the result of that trial "would have been different" than the result of the plea bargain. . . . We instead consider whether the defendant was prejudiced by the "denial of the entire judicial proceeding . . . to which he had a right." [When] a defendant claims that his counsel's deficient performance deprived him of a trial by causing him to accept a plea, the defendant can show prejudice by demonstrating a reasonable probability that, but for counsel's errors, he would not have pleaded guilty and would have insisted on going to trial.

The dissent contends that a defendant must also show that he would have been better off going to trial. That is true when the defendant's decision about going to trial turns on his prospects of success and those are affected by the attorney's error—for instance, where a defendant alleges that his lawyer should have but did not seek to suppress an improperly obtained confession. Premo v. Moore, 562 U.S. 115 (2011).

Not all errors, however, are of that sort. Here Lee knew, correctly, that his prospects of acquittal at trial were grim, and his attorney's error had nothing to do with that. The error was instead one that affected Lee's understanding of the consequences of pleading guilty. The Court confronted precisely this kind of error in Hill v. Lockhart, 474 U.S. 52 (1985). Rather than asking how a hypothetical trial would have played out absent the error, the Court considered whether there was an adequate showing that the defendant, properly advised, would have opted to go to trial. The Court rejected the defendant's claim because he had "alleged no special circumstances that might support the conclusion that he placed particular emphasis on his parole eligibility in deciding whether or not to plead guilty."

Lee, on the other hand, argues he can establish prejudice under *Hill* because he never would have accepted a guilty plea had he known that he would be deported as a result. Lee insists he would have gambled on trial, risking more jail time for whatever small chance there might be of an acquittal that would let him remain in the United States. The Government responds that, since Lee had no viable defense at trial, he would almost certainly have lost and found himself still subject to deportation, with a lengthier prison sentence to boot. Lee, the Government contends, cannot show prejudice from accepting a plea where his only hope at trial was that something unexpected and unpredictable might occur that would lead to an acquittal.

B.

The Government asks that we . . . adopt a per se rule that a defendant with no viable defense cannot show prejudice from the denial of his right to trial. As a general matter, it makes sense that a defendant who has no realistic defense to a charge supported by sufficient evidence will be unable to carry his burden of showing prejudice from accepting a guilty plea. But in elevating this general proposition to a per se rule, the Government makes two errors. First, it forgets that categorical rules are ill suited to an inquiry that we have emphasized demands a "case-by-case examination" of the "totality of the evidence." And, more fundamentally, the Government overlooks that the inquiry we prescribed in *Hill* focuses on a defendant's decisionmaking, which may not turn solely on the likelihood of conviction after trial.

A defendant without any viable defense will be highly likely to lose at trial. And a defendant facing such long odds will rarely be able to show prejudice from accepting a guilty plea that offers him a better resolution than would be likely after trial. But that is not because the prejudice inquiry in this context looks to the probability of a conviction for its own sake. It is instead because defendants obviously weigh their prospects at trial in deciding whether to accept a plea. Where a defendant has no plausible chance of an acquittal at trial, it is highly likely that he will accept a plea if the Government offers one.

But common sense (not to mention our precedent) recognizes that there is more to consider than simply the likelihood of success at trial. The decision whether to plead guilty also involves assessing the respective consequences of a conviction after trial and by plea. See INS v. St. Cyr, 533 U.S. 289 (2001). When those consequences are, from the defendant's perspective, similarly dire, even the smallest chance of success at trial may look attractive. For example, a defendant with no realistic defense to a charge carrying a 20-year sentence may nevertheless choose trial, if the prosecution's plea offer is 18 years. Here Lee alleges that avoiding deportation was the determinative factor for him; deportation after some time in prison was not meaningfully different from deportation after somewhat less time. He says he accordingly would have rejected any plea leading to deportation—even if it shaved off prison time—in favor of throwing a "Hail Mary" at trial. . . .

C.

"Surmounting *Strickland*'s high bar is never an easy task," Padilla v. Kentucky, 559 U.S. 356 (2010), and the strong societal interest in finality has "special force with respect to convictions based on guilty pleas." Courts should not upset a plea solely because of post hoc assertions from a defendant about how he would have pleaded but for his attorney's deficiencies. Judges should instead look to contemporaneous evidence to substantiate a defendant's expressed preferences.

In the unusual circumstances of this case, we conclude that Lee has adequately demonstrated a reasonable probability that he would have rejected the plea had he known that it would lead to mandatory deportation. There is no question that deportation was the determinative issue in Lee's decision whether to accept the plea deal. Lee asked his attorney repeatedly whether there was any risk of deportation from the proceedings, and both Lee and his attorney testified at the evidentiary hearing below that Lee would have gone to trial if he had known about the deportation consequences.

Lee demonstrated as much at his plea colloquy: When the judge warned him that a conviction "could result in your being deported," and asked "does that at all affect your decision about whether you want to plead guilty or not," Lee answered "Yes, Your Honor." When the judge inquired "how does it affect your decision," Lee responded "I don't understand," and turned to his attorney for advice. Only when Lee's counsel assured him that the judge's statement was a "standard warning" was Lee willing to proceed to plead guilty.

There is no reason to doubt the paramount importance Lee placed on avoiding deportation. . . . At the time of his plea, Lee had lived in the United States for nearly three decades, had established two businesses in Tennessee, and was the only family member in the United States who could care for his elderly parents—both naturalized American citizens. In contrast to these strong connections to the United States, there is no indication that he had any ties to South Korea; he had never returned there since leaving as a child.

The Government argues, however, that under Padilla v. Kentucky, a defendant "must convince the court that a decision to reject the plea bargain would have been rational under the circumstances." The Government contends that Lee cannot make that showing because he was going to be deported either way; going to trial would only result in a longer sentence before that inevitable consequence.

We cannot agree that it would be irrational for a defendant in Lee's position to reject the plea offer in favor of trial. But for his attorney's incompetence, Lee would have known that accepting the plea agreement would certainly lead to deportation. Going to trial? Almost certainly. If deportation were the "determinative issue" for an individual in plea discussions, as it was for Lee; if that individual had strong connections to this country and no other, as did Lee; and if the consequences of taking a chance at trial were not markedly harsher than pleading, as in this case, that "almost" could make all the difference. Balanced against holding on to some chance of avoiding deportation was a year or two more of prison time. Not everyone in Lee's position would make the choice to reject the plea. But we cannot say it would be irrational to do so. . . .

THOMAS, J., dissenting.

. . . When the Court extended the right to effective counsel to the plea stage, see Hill v. Lockhart, 474 U.S. 52 (1985), it held that "the same two-part standard" from *Strickland* applies. To be sure, the Court said—and the majority today emphasizes—that a defendant asserting an ineffectiveness claim at the plea stage "must show that there is a reasonable probability that, but for counsel's errors, he would not have pleaded guilty and would have insisted on going to trial." But that requirement merely reflects the reality that a defendant cannot show that the outcome of his case would have been different if he would have accepted his current plea anyway. In other words, the defendant's ability to show that he would have gone to trial is necessary, but not sufficient, to establish prejudice.

The *Hill* Court went on to explain that *Strickland*'s two-part test applies the same way in the plea context as in other contexts. In particular, the "assessment" will primarily turn on "a prediction whether," in the absence of counsel's error, "the evidence" of the defendant's innocence or guilt "likely would have changed the outcome" of the proceeding. Thus, a defendant cannot show prejudice where it is "inconceivable" not only that he would have gone to trial, but also "that if he had done so he either would have been acquitted or, if convicted, would nevertheless have been given a shorter sentence than he actually received." In sum, the proper inquiry requires a defendant to show both that he would have rejected his plea and gone to trial and that he would likely have obtained a more favorable result in the end. . . .

The majority today abandons any pretense of applying *Strickland* to claims of ineffective assistance of counsel that arise at the plea stage. It instead concludes that one standard applies when a defendant goes to trial (*Strickland*); another standard applies when a defendant accepts a plea (*Hill*); and yet another standard applies when counsel does not apprise the defendant of an available plea or when the defendant rejects a plea (*Frye* and *Lafler*). That approach leaves little doubt that the Court has [opened] a whole new field of constitutionalized criminal procedure—"plea-bargaining law"—despite its repeated assurances that it has been applying the same *Strickland* standard all along. In my view, we should take the Court's precedents at their word and conclude that an error by counsel . . . "does not warrant setting aside the judgment of a criminal proceeding if the error had no effect on the judgment.". . .

The Court's decision today will have pernicious consequences for the criminal justice system. This Court has shown special solicitude for the plea process, which brings "stability" and "certainty" to the criminal justice system. The Court has warned that "the prospect of collateral challenges" threatens to undermine these important values. And we have explained that prosecutors "must have assurance that a plea will not be undone years later," lest they "forgo plea bargains that would benefit defendants," which would be "a result favorable to no one."

The Court today provides no assurance that plea deals negotiated in good faith with guilty defendants will remain final. For one thing, the Court's artificially cabined standard for prejudice in the plea context is likely to generate a high volume of challenges to existing and future plea agreements. Under the majority's standard, defendants bringing these challenges will bear a relatively low burden to show prejudice. Whereas a defendant asserting an ordinary claim of ineffective assistance of counsel must prove that the ultimate outcome of his case would have been different, the Court today holds that a defendant who pleaded guilty need show only that he would have rejected his plea and gone to trial. This standard does not appear to be particularly demanding, as even a defendant who has only the "smallest chance of success at trial"—relying on nothing more than a "Hail Mary"—may be able to satisfy it. For another, the Court does not limit its holding to immigration consequences. Under its rule, so long as a defendant alleges that his counsel omitted or misadvised him on a piece of information during the plea process that he considered of "paramount importance," he could allege a plausible claim of ineffective assistance of counsel.

In addition to undermining finality, the Court's rule will impose significant costs on courts and prosecutors. Under the Court's standard, a challenge to a guilty plea will be a highly fact-intensive, defendant-specific undertaking. Petitioner suggests that each claim will "at least" require a "hearing to get [the] facts on the table." Given that more than 90 percent of criminal convictions are the result of guilty pleas, the burden of holding evidentiary hearings on these claims could be significant. In circumstances where a defendant has admitted his guilt, the evidence against him is overwhelming, and he has no bona fide defense strategy, I see no justification for imposing these costs. . . .

B. Categorical Restrictions on Bargaining

3. Prosecutorial Guidelines

Page 1117. Place this material at the end of note 1.

The latest pendulum swing in policy for the Department of Justice in selecting charges and recommending sentences appears in a May 2017 announcement from Attorney General Jeff Sessions. That policy is reprinted in Chapter 13 of this Supplement.

C. Validity of Individual Plea Bargains

2. Involuntary Pleas

Page 1158. Place this material at the end of note 4.

One could also characterize judicial involvement in plea negotiations as a counterweight to coercive prosecutor tactics in charging. Judge Jed Rakoff makes the following proposal for a new process in federal court:

> As I envision it, shortly after an indictment is returned (or perhaps even earlier if an arrest has occurred and the defendant is jailed), a magistrate would meet separately with the prosecutor and the defense counsel, in proceedings that would be recorded but placed under seal, and all present would be provided with the particulars regarding the evidence and issues in the case. In certain circumstances, the magistrate might interview witnesses or examine other evidence, again under seal so as not to compromise any party's strategy. He might even interview the defendant, under an arrangement where it would not constitute a waiver of the defendant's Fifth Amendment privilege against self-incrimination.
>
> The prosecutor would, in the meantime, be precluded from making any plea bargain offer (or threat) while the magistrate was studying the case. Once the magistrate was ready, he would then meet separately with both sides and, if appropriate, make a recommendation, such as to dismiss the case (if he thought the proof was weak), to proceed to trial (if he thought there was no reasonable plea bargain available), or to enter into a plea bargain along lines the magistrate might suggest. No party would be required to follow the magistrate's suggestions. Their force, if any, would come from the fact that they were being suggested by a neutral third party, who, moreover, was a judicial officer that the prosecutors and the defense lawyers would have to appear before in many other cases.

Jed S. Rakoff, Why Innocent People Plead Guilty, N.Y. Review of Books, Nov. 20, 2014.

Chapter 17

Decisionmakers at Trial

B. Selection of Jurors

1. Voir Dire

Page 1198. Place this material at the end of note 1.

See also Cynthia Lee, A New Approach to Voir Dire on Racial Bias, 5 U.C. Irvine L. Rev. 843 (2015).

2. Dismissal for Cause

Page 1205. Place this material at the end of note 3.

See also White v. Wheeler, 136 S. Ct. 456 (2015) (substantial deference that federal courts must give to state-court rulings in habeas proceedings prevented court from granting relief based on dismissal of juror in the circumstances of this case).

3. Peremptory Challenges

Page 1220. Place this material before the Notes.

Timothy Tyrone Foster v. Bruce Chatman
136 S. Ct. 1737 (2016)

ROBERTS, C.J.*

Petitioner Timothy Foster was convicted of capital murder and sentenced to death in a Georgia court. During jury selection at his trial, the State exercised peremptory strikes against all four black prospective jurors qualified to serve. Foster argued that the State's use of those strikes was racially motivated, in violation of our decision in Batson v. Kentucky, 476 U.S. 79 (1986). The trial court and the Georgia Supreme Court rejected Foster's *Batson* claim. Foster then sought a writ of habeas corpus from the Superior Court of Butts County, Georgia, renewing his *Batson* objection. That court denied relief, and the Georgia Supreme Court declined to issue the Certificate of Probable Cause necessary under Georgia law for Foster to pursue an appeal. We granted certiorari and now reverse.

I.

On the morning of August 28, 1986, police found Queen Madge White dead on the floor of her home in Rome, Georgia. White, a 79-year-old widow, had been beaten, sexually assaulted, and strangled to death. Her home had been burglarized. Timothy Foster subsequently confessed to killing White, and White's possessions were recovered from Foster's home and from Foster's two sisters. The State indicted Foster on charges of malice murder and burglary. He faced the death penalty.

District Attorney Stephen Lanier and Assistant District Attorney Douglas Pullen represented the State at trial. Jury selection proceeded in two phases: removals for cause and peremptory strikes. In the first phase, each prospective juror completed a detailed questionnaire, which the prosecution and defense reviewed. The trial court then conducted a juror-by-juror *voir dire* of approximately 90 prospective jurors. Throughout this process, both parties had the opportunity to question the prospective

* [Justices Kennedy, Ginsburg, Breyer, Sotomayor, and Kagan joined this opinion—EDS.]

jurors and lodge challenges for cause. This first phase whittled the list down to 42 "qualified" prospective jurors. Five were black.

In the second phase, known as the "striking of the jury," both parties had the opportunity to exercise peremptory strikes against the array of qualified jurors. Pursuant to state law, the prosecution had ten such strikes; Foster twenty. See Ga. Code Ann. § 15-12-165 (1985). The process worked as follows: The clerk of the court called the qualified prospective jurors one by one, and the State had the option to exercise one of its peremptory strikes. If the State declined to strike a particular prospective juror, Foster then had the opportunity to do so. If neither party exercised a peremptory strike, the prospective juror was selected for service. This second phase continued until 12 jurors had been accepted.

The morning the second phase began, Shirley Powell, one of the five qualified black prospective jurors, notified the court that she had just learned that one of her close friends was related to Foster. The court removed Powell for cause. That left four black prospective jurors: Eddie Hood, Evelyn Hardge, Mary Turner, and Marilyn Garrett.

The striking of the jury then commenced. The State exercised nine of its ten allotted peremptory strikes, removing all four of the remaining black prospective jurors. Foster immediately lodged a *Batson* challenge. The trial court rejected the objection and empaneled the jury. The jury convicted Foster and sentenced him to death.

Following sentencing, Foster renewed his *Batson* claim in a motion for a new trial. After an evidentiary hearing, the trial court denied the motion. The Georgia Supreme Court affirmed, and we denied certiorari.

Foster subsequently sought a writ of habeas corpus from the Superior Court of Butts County, Georgia, again pressing his *Batson* claim. While the state habeas proceeding was pending, Foster filed a series of requests under the Georgia Open Records Act, see Ga. Code Ann. §§ 50-18-70 to 50-18-77, seeking access to the State's file from his 1987 trial. In response, the State disclosed documents related to the jury selection at that trial. Over the State's objections, the state habeas court admitted those documents into evidence. They included the following:

(1) Four copies of the jury venire list. On each copy, the names of the black prospective jurors were highlighted in bright green. A legend in the upper right corner of the lists indicated that the green highlighting "represents Blacks." The letter "B" also appeared next to each black prospective juror's name. According to the testimony of Clayton Lundy,

an investigator who assisted the prosecution during jury selection, these highlighted venire lists were circulated in the district attorney's office during jury selection. That allowed "everybody in the office"—approximately "10 to 12 people," including "secretaries, investigators, and district attorneys"—to look at them, share information, and contribute thoughts on whether the prosecution should strike a particular juror. The documents, Lundy testified, were returned to Lanier before jury selection.

(2) A draft of an affidavit that had been prepared by Lundy "at Lanier's request" for submission to the state trial court in response to Foster's motion for a new trial. The typed draft detailed Lundy's views on ten black prospective jurors, stating "[m]y evaluation of the jurors are a[s] follows." Under the name of one of those jurors, Lundy had written:

> If it comes down to having to pick one of the black jurors, [this one] might be okay. This is solely my opinion. . .. Upon picking of the jury after listening to all of the jurors we had to pick, if we had to pick a black juror I recommend that [this juror] be one of the jurors.

That text had been crossed out by hand; the version of the affidavit filed with the trial court did not contain the crossed-out language. Lundy testified that he "guessed" the redactions had been done by Lanier.

(3) Three handwritten notes on black prospective jurors Eddie Hood, Louise Wilson, and Corrie Hinds. Annotations denoted those individuals as "B # 1," "B# 2," and "B# 3," respectively. Lundy testified that these were examples of the type of "notes that the team—the State would take down during voir dire to help select the jury in Mr. Foster's case."

(4) A typed list of the qualified jurors remaining after *voir dire*. It included "Ns" next to ten jurors' names, which Lundy told the state habeas court "signified the ten jurors that the State had strikes for during jury selection." Such an "N" appeared alongside the names of all five qualified black prospective jurors. The file also included a handwritten version of the same list, with the same markings. Lundy testified that he was unsure who had prepared or marked the two lists.

(5) A handwritten document titled "definite NO's," listing six names. The first five were those of the five qualified black prospective jurors. The State concedes that either Lanier or Pullen compiled the list, which Lundy testified was "used for preparation in jury selection."

(6) A handwritten document titled "Church of Christ." A notation

on the document read: "*NO*. No *Black* Church."

(7) The questionnaires that had been completed by several of the black prospective jurors. On each one, the juror's response indicating his or her race had been circled.

In response to the admission of this evidence, the State introduced short affidavits from Lanier and Pullen. Lanier's affidavit stated:

> I did not make any of the highlighted marks on the jury venire list. It was common practice in the office to highlight in yellow those jurors who had prior case experience. I did not instruct anyone to make the green highlighted marks. I reaffirm my testimony made during the motion for new trial hearing as to how I used my peremptory jury strikes and the basis and reasons for those strikes.

Pullen's affidavit averred:

> I did not make any of the highlighted marks on the jury venire list, and I did not instruct anyone else to make the highlighted marks. I did not rely on the highlighted jury venire list in making my decision on how to use my peremptory strikes.

Neither affidavit provided further explanation of the documents, and neither Lanier nor Pullen testified in the habeas proceeding.

After considering the evidence, the state habeas court denied relief. The court first stated that, as a preliminary matter, Foster's *Batson* claim was "not reviewable based on the doctrine of res judicata" because it had been "raised and litigated adversely to [Foster] on his direct appeal to the Georgia Supreme Court." The court nonetheless announced that it would make findings of fact and conclusions of law on that claim. Based on what it referred to as a "*Batson* . . . analysis," the court concluded that Foster's "renewed *Batson* claim is without merit," because he had "failed to demonstrate purposeful discrimination." The Georgia Supreme Court denied Foster the "Certificate of Probable Cause" necessary under state law for him to pursue an appeal, determining that his claim had no "arguable merit." We granted certiorari. . . .

III.

A.

The "Constitution forbids striking even a single prospective juror for a discriminatory purpose." Snyder v. Louisiana, 552 U.S. 472 (2008).

Our decision in Batson v. Kentucky, 476 U.S. 79, provides a three-step process for determining when a strike is discriminatory:

> First, a defendant must make a prima facie showing that a peremptory challenge has been exercised on the basis of race; second, if that showing has been made, the prosecution must offer a race-neutral basis for striking the juror in question; and third, in light of the parties' submissions, the trial court must determine whether the defendant has shown purposeful discrimination."

Both parties agree that Foster has demonstrated a prima facie case, and that the prosecutors have offered race-neutral reasons for their strikes. We therefore address only *Batson*'s third step. That step turns on factual determinations, and, "in the absence of exceptional circumstances," we defer to state court factual findings unless we conclude that they are clearly erroneous.

Before reviewing the factual record in this case, a brief word is in order regarding the contents of the prosecution's file that Foster obtained through his Georgia Open Records Act requests. Pursuant to those requests, Foster received a "certified . . . true and correct copy of 103 pages of the State's case file" from his 1987 trial. The State argues that "because [Foster] did not call either of the prosecutors to the stand" to testify in his state habeas proceedings, "he can only speculate as to the meaning of various markings and writings" on those pages, "the author of many of them, and whether the two prosecutors at trial (District Attorney Lanier and Assistant District Attorney Pullen) even saw many of them." For these reasons, the State argues, "none of the specific pieces of new evidence [found in the file] shows an intent to discriminate." For his part, Foster argues that "there is no question that the prosecutors used the lists and notes, which came from the prosecution's file and were certified as such," and therefore the "source of the lists and notes, their timing, and their purpose is hardly 'unknown' or based on 'conjecture.'"

The State concedes that the prosecutors themselves authored some documents, and Lundy's testimony strongly suggests that the prosecutors viewed others. There are, however, genuine questions that remain about the provenance of other documents. Nothing in the record, for example, identifies the author of the notes that listed three black prospective jurors as "B# 1," "B# 2," and "B# 3." Such notes, then, are not necessarily attributable directly to the prosecutors themselves. The state habeas court was cognizant of those limitations, but nevertheless admitted the file into evidence, reserving "a determination as to what weight the Court is going to put on any of [them]" in light of the objections urged by the State.

We agree with that approach. Despite questions about the background of particular notes, we cannot accept the State's invitation to blind ourselves to their existence. We have made it clear that in considering a *Batson* objection, or in reviewing a ruling claimed to be *Batson* error, all of the circumstances that bear upon the issue of racial animosity must be consulted. . . . At a minimum, we are comfortable that all documents in the file were authored by *someone* in the district attorney's office. Any uncertainties concerning the documents are pertinent only as potential limits on their probative value.

B.

Foster centers his *Batson* claim on the strikes of two black prospective jurors, Marilyn Garrett and Eddie Hood. We turn first to Marilyn Garrett. According to Lanier, on the morning that the State was to use its strikes he had not yet made up his mind to remove Garrett. Rather, he decided to strike her only after learning that he would not need to use a strike on another black prospective juror, Shirley Powell, who was excused for cause that morning.

Ultimately, Lanier did strike Garrett. In justifying that strike to the trial court, he articulated a laundry list of reasons. Specifically, Lanier objected to Garrett because she: (1) worked with disadvantaged youth in her job as a teacher's aide; (2) kept looking at the ground during *voir dire*; (3) gave short and curt answers during *voir dire*; (4) appeared nervous; (5) was too young; (6) misrepresented her familiarity with the location of the crime; (7) failed to disclose that her cousin had been arrested on a drug charge; (8) was divorced; (9) had two children and two jobs; (10) was asked few questions by the defense; and (11) did not ask to be excused from jury service.

The trial court accepted Lanier's justifications, concluding that "in the totality of circumstances," there was "no discriminatory intent, and that there existed reasonably clear, specific, and legitimate reasons" for the strike. On their face, Lanier's justifications for the strike seem reasonable enough. Our independent examination of the record, however, reveals that much of the reasoning provided by Lanier has no grounding in fact.

Lanier's misrepresentations to the trial court began with an elaborate explanation of how he ultimately came to strike Garrett:

> The prosecution considered this juror [to have] the most potential to choose from out of the four remaining blacks in the 42 [member] panel venire. However, a system of events took place on the morning of jury selection that caused the excusal of this juror. The State had, in his jury notes, *listed this juror as questionable*. The four negative challenges were allocated for Hardge, Hood, Turner and Powell. . .. But on the morning of jury selection, Juror Powell was excused for cause with no objections by defense counsel. She was replaced by Juror Cadle [who] was acceptable to the State. This left the State with an additional strike it had not anticipated or allocated. Consequently, the State had to choose between [white] Juror Blackmon or Juror Garrett, the only two *questionable* jurors the State had left on the list.

Lanier then offered an extensive list of reasons for striking Garrett and explained that "these factors, with no reference to race, were considered by the prosecutor in this particular case to result in a juror less desirable from the prosecutor's viewpoint than Juror Blackmon." Lanier then compared Blackmon to Garrett. In contrast to Garrett, Juror Blackmon

> was 46 years old, married 13 years to her husband who works at GE, buying her own home and [was recommended by a third party to] this prosecutor. She was no longer employed at Northwest Georgia Regional Hospital and she attended Catholic church on an irregular basis. She did not hesitate when answering the questions concerning the death penalty, had good eye contact with the prosecutor and gave good answers on the insanity issue. She was perceived by the prosecutor as having a stable home environment, of the right age and no association with any disadvantaged youth organizations.

Lanier concluded that "the chances of [Blackmon] returning a death sentence were greater when all these factors were considered than Juror Garrett. Consequently, Juror Garrett was excused."

The trial court accepted this explanation in denying Foster's motion for a new trial. But the predicate for the State's account—that Garrett was "listed" by the prosecution as "questionable," making that strike a last-minute race-neutral decision—was false.

During jury selection, the State went first. As a consequence, the defense could accept any prospective juror not struck by the State without any further opportunity for the State to use a strike against that prospective juror. Accordingly, the State had to "pretty well select the ten specific people [it] intended to strike" in advance. The record evidence shows that Garrett was one of those "ten specific people."

That much is evident from the "definite NO's" list in the prosecution's file. Garrett's name appeared on that list, which the State concedes was written by one of the prosecutors. That list belies Lanier's assertion that the State considered allowing Garrett to serve. The title of the list meant what it said: Garrett was a "*definite* NO." The State from the outset was intent on ensuring that *none* of the jurors on that list would serve.

The first five names on the "definite NO's" list were Eddie Hood, Evelyn Hardge, Shirley Powell, Marilyn Garrett, and Mary Turner. All were black. The State struck each one except Powell (who, as discussed, was excused for cause at the last minute—though the prosecution informed the trial court that the "State was not, under any circumstances, going to take [Powell]." Only in the number six position did a white prospective juror appear, and she had informed the court during *voir dire* that she could not "say positively" that she could impose the death penalty even if the evidence warranted it. In short, contrary to the prosecution's submissions, the State's resolve to strike Garrett was never in doubt.

The State attempts to explain away the contradiction between the "definite NO's" list and Lanier's statements to the trial court as an example of a prosecutor merely "misspeaking." But this was not some off-the-cuff remark; it was an intricate story expounded by the prosecution in writing, laid out over three single-spaced pages in a brief filed with the trial court.

Moreover, several of Lanier's reasons for *why* he chose Garrett over Blackmon are similarly contradicted by the record. Lanier told the court, for example, that he struck Garrett because "the defense did not ask her questions about" pertinent trial issues such as her thoughts on "insanity" or "alcohol," or "much questions on publicity." But the trial transcripts reveal that the defense asked her several questions on all three topics.

Still other explanations given by the prosecution, while not explicitly contradicted by the record, are difficult to credit because the State willingly accepted white jurors with the same traits that supposedly rendered Garrett an unattractive juror. Lanier told the trial court that he struck Garrett because she was divorced. But he declined to strike three out of the four prospective white jurors who were also divorced. Additionally, Lanier claimed that he struck Garrett because she was too young, and the "State was looking for older jurors that would not easily identify with the defendant." Yet Garrett was 34, and the State declined to strike eight white prospective jurors under the age of 36. Two of those white jurors served on the jury; one of those two was only 21 years old.

Lanier also explained to the trial court that he struck Garrett because he "felt that she was less than truthful" in her answers in *voir dire*. Specifically, the State pointed the trial court to the following exchange:

> [Court]: Are you familiar with the neighborhood where [the victim] lived, North Rome?
> [Garrett]: No.

Lanier, in explaining the strike, told the trial court that in apparent contradiction to that exchange (which represented the only time that Garrett was asked about the topic during *voir dire*), he had "noted that [Garrett] attended Main High School, which is only two blocks from where [the victim] lived and certainly in the neighborhood. She denied any knowledge of the area."

We have no quarrel with the State's general assertion that it "could not trust someone who gave materially untruthful answers on voir dire." But even this otherwise legitimate reason is difficult to credit in light of the State's acceptance of (white) juror Duncan. Duncan gave practically the same answer as Garrett did during *voir dire*:

> [Court]: Are you familiar with the neighborhood in which [the victim] lived?
> [Duncan]: No. I live in Atteiram Heights, but it's not—I'm not familiar with up there, you know.

But, as Lanier was aware, Duncan's residence was less than a half a mile from the murder scene and her workplace was located less than 250 yards away. In sum, in evaluating the strike of Garrett, we are not faced with a single isolated misrepresentation.

C.

We turn next to the strike of Hood. According to Lanier, Hood "was exactly what [the State] was looking for in terms of age, between forty and fifty, good employment and married." The prosecution nonetheless struck Hood, giving eight reasons for doing so. Hood: (1) had a son who was the same age as the defendant and who had previously been convicted of a crime; (2) had a wife who worked in food service at the local mental health institution; (3) had experienced food poisoning during *voir dire*; (4) was slow in responding to death penalty questions; (5) was a member of the Church of Christ; (6) had a brother who counseled drug offenders; (7) was not asked enough questions by the defense during *voir dire*; and (8) asked to be excused from jury service. An examination of the record, however, convinces us that many of these justifications cannot be credited.

As an initial matter, the prosecution's principal reasons for the strike shifted over time, suggesting that those reasons may be pretextual. In response to Foster's pre-trial *Batson* challenge, District Attorney Lanier noted all eight reasons, but explained:

> *The only thing I was concerned about,* and I will state it for the record. He has an eighteen year old son which is about the same age as the defendant. In my experience prosecuting over twenty-five murder cases . . . individuals having the same son as [a] defendant who is charged with murder [have] serious reservations and are more sympathetic and lean toward that particular person. It is ironic that his son, . . . Darrell Hood, has been sentenced . . . by the Court here, to theft by taking on April 4th, 1982. . .. Theft by taking is basically the same thing that this defendant is charged with.

But by the time of Foster's subsequent motion for a new trial, Lanier's focus had shifted. He still noted the similarities between Hood's son and Foster, but that was no longer the key reason behind the strike. Lanier instead told the court that his paramount concern was Hood's membership in the Church of Christ: "The Church of Christ people, while they may not take a formal stand against the death penalty, they are very, very reluctant to vote for the death penalty." Hood's religion, Lanier now explained, was the most important factor behind the strike: "I evaluated the whole Eddie Hood. . . . And *the bottom line* on Eddie Hood is the Church of Christ affiliation."

Of course it is possible that Lanier simply misspoke in one of the two proceedings. But even if that were so, we would expect at least *one* of the two purportedly principal justifications for the strike to withstand closer scrutiny. Neither does.

Take Hood's son. If Darrell Hood's age was the issue, why did the State accept (white) juror Billy Graves, who had a 17-year-old son? And why did the State accept (white) juror Martha Duncan, even though she had a 20-year-old son?

The comparison between Hood and Graves is particularly salient. When the prosecution asked Hood if Foster's age would be a factor for him in sentencing, he answered "None whatsoever." Graves, on the other hand, answered the same question "probably so." Yet the State struck Hood and accepted Graves.

The State responds that Duncan and Graves were not similar to Hood because Hood's son had been convicted of theft, while Graves's and Duncan's sons had not. Lanier had described Darrell Hood's conviction to the trial court as being for "basically the same thing that this defendant is charged with." Nonsense. Hood's son had received a 12-month suspended sentence for stealing hubcaps from a car in a mall parking lot five years earlier. Foster was charged with capital murder of a 79-year-old widow after a brutal sexual assault. The "implausible" and "fantastic" assertion that the two had been charged with "basically the same thing" supports our conclusion that the focus on Hood's son can only be regarded as pretextual. Miller-El v. Cockrell, 537 U.S. 322 (2003).

The prosecution's second principal justification for striking Hood—his affiliation with the Church of Christ, and that church's alleged teachings on the death penalty—fares no better. Hood asserted no fewer than four times during *voir dire* that he could impose the death penalty. A prosecutor is entitled to disbelieve a juror's *voir dire* answers, of course. But the record persuades us that Hood's race, and not his religious affiliation, was Lanier's true motivation.

The first indication to that effect is Lanier's mischaracterization of the record. On multiple occasions, Lanier asserted to the trial court that three white prospective jurors who were members of the Church of Christ had been struck for cause due to their opposition to the death penalty.

That was not true. One of those prospective jurors was excused before even being questioned during *voir dire* because she was five-and-a-half months pregnant. Another was excused by the agreement of both parties because her answers on the death penalty made it difficult to ascertain her precise views on capital punishment. And the judge found cause to dismiss the third because she had already formed an opinion about Foster's guilt.

The prosecution's file fortifies our conclusion that any reliance on Hood's religion was pretextual. The file contains a handwritten document titled "Church of Christ." The document notes that the church "doesn't take a stand on [the] Death Penalty," and that the issue is "left for each individual member." The document then states: "*NO*. NO *Black* Church." The State tries to downplay the significance of this document by emphasizing that the document's author is unknown. That uncertainty is pertinent. But we think the document is nonetheless entitled to significant weight, especially given that it is consistent with our serious doubts about the prosecution's account of the strike.

Many of the State's secondary justifications similarly come undone when subjected to scrutiny. Lanier told the trial court that Hood "appeared to be confused and slow in responding to questions concerning his views on the death penalty." As previously noted, however, Hood unequivocally voiced his willingness to impose the death penalty, and a white juror who showed similar confusion served on the jury. According to the record, such confusion was not uncommon.

Lanier also stated that he struck Hood because Hood's wife worked at Northwest Regional Hospital as a food services supervisor. That hospital, Lanier explained, "deals a lot with mentally disturbed, mentally ill people," and so people associated with it tend "to be more sympathetic to the underdog." But Lanier expressed no such concerns about white juror Blackmon, who had worked at the same hospital. Blackmon, as noted, served on the jury.

Lanier additionally stated that he struck Hood because the defense "didn't ask [Hood] any questions about the age of the defendant," "his feelings about criminal responsibility involved in insanity," or "publicity." Yet again, the trial transcripts clearly indicate the contrary.

D.

As we explained in *Miller-El v. Dretke,* "if a prosecutor's proffered reason for striking a black panelist applies just as well to an otherwise-similar nonblack [panelist] who is permitted to serve, that is evidence tending to prove purposeful discrimination." 545 U.S. 231 (2005). With respect to both Garrett and Hood, such evidence is compelling. But that is not all. There are also the shifting explanations, the misrepresentations of the record, and the persistent focus on race in the prosecution's file. Considering all of the circumstantial evidence that "bears upon the issue of racial animosity," we are left with the firm conviction that the strikes of Garrett and Hood were "motivated in substantial part by discriminatory intent."

Throughout all stages of this litigation, the State has strenuously objected that "race [was] not a factor" in its jury selection strategy. Indeed, at times the State has been downright indignant.

The contents of the prosecution's file, however, plainly belie the State's claim that it exercised its strikes in a "color-blind" manner. The sheer number of references to race in that file is arresting. The State, however, claims that things are not quite as bad as they seem. The focus on black prospective jurors, it contends, does not indicate any attempt to exclude them from the jury. It instead reflects an effort to ensure that the State was "thoughtful and non-discriminatory in [its] consideration of black prospective jurors [and] to develop and maintain detailed information on those prospective jurors in order to properly defend against any suggestion that decisions regarding [its] selections were pretextual." *Batson,* after all, had come down only months before Foster's trial. The prosecutors, according to the State, were uncertain what sort of showing might be demanded of them and wanted to be prepared.

This argument falls flat. To begin, it "reeks of afterthought," having never before been made in the nearly 30-year history of this litigation: not in the trial court, not in the state habeas court, and not even in the State's brief in opposition to Foster's petition for certiorari.

In addition, the focus on race in the prosecution's file plainly demonstrates a concerted effort to keep black prospective jurors off the jury. The State argues that it "was actively seeking a black juror." But this claim is not credible. An "N" appeared next to each of the black prospective jurors' names on the jury venire list. An "N" was also noted next to the name of each black prospective juror on the list of the 42 qualified prospective jurors; each of those names also appeared on the "definite NO's" list. And a draft affidavit from the prosecution's investigator stated his view that "if it comes down to *having to pick* one of the black jurors, [Marilyn] Garrett, might be okay." Such references are inconsistent with attempts to "actively see[k]" a black juror.

The State's new argument today does not dissuade us from the conclusion that its prosecutors were motivated in substantial part by race when they struck Garrett and Hood from the jury 30 years ago. Two peremptory strikes on the basis of race are two more than the Constitution allows. . . .

ALITO, J., concurring in the judgment.

. . . I agree with the Court that the totality of the evidence now adduced by Foster is sufficient to make out a *Batson* violation. On remand, the Georgia Supreme Court is bound to accept that evaluation of the federal question, but whether that conclusion justifies relief under state res judicata law is a matter for that court to decide.

Compliance with *Batson* is essential to ensure that defendants receive a fair trial and to preserve the public confidence upon which our system of criminal justice depends. But it is also important that this Court respect the authority of state courts to structure their systems of post-conviction review in a way that promotes the expeditious and definitive disposition of claims of error.

Until recently, this Court rarely granted review of state-court decisions in collateral review proceedings, preferring to allow the claims adjudicated in such proceedings to be decided first in federal habeas proceedings. When cases reach this Court after habeas review in the lower federal courts, the standards of review set out in the Antiterrorism and Effective Death Penalty Act of 1996, 28 U.S.C. § 2254, apply. Recently, this Court has evidenced a predilection for granting review of state-court decisions denying post-conviction relief. Particularly in light of that trend, it is important that we do not lightly brush aside the States' legitimate interest in structuring their systems of post-conviction review in a way that militates against repetitive litigation and endless delay.

THOMAS, J., dissenting.

Thirty years ago, Timothy Foster confessed to murdering Queen Madge White after sexually assaulting her with a bottle of salad dressing. In the decades since, Foster has sought to vacate his conviction and death sentence on the ground that prosecutors violated Batson v. Kentucky when they struck all black prospective jurors before his trial. Time and again, the state courts have rejected that claim. The trial court twice rejected it, and the Supreme Court of Georgia unequivocally rejected it when Foster directly appealed his conviction and sentence. A state habeas court rejected it in 2013. And most recently, the Supreme Court of Georgia again rejected it as lacking "arguable merit." . . .

Because the adjudication of his *Batson* claim is, at bottom, a credibility determination, we owe "great deference" to the state court's initial finding that the prosecution's race-neutral reasons for striking veniremen Eddie Hood and Marilyn Garrett were credible. . . .

By allowing Foster to re-litigate his *Batson* claim by bringing this newly discovered evidence to the fore, the Court upends *Batson*'s deferential framework. Foster's new evidence does not justify this Court's reassessment of who was telling the truth nearly three decades removed from *voir dire*. . . .

The Court today invites state prisoners to go searching for new "evidence" by demanding the files of the prosecutors who long ago convicted them. If those prisoners succeed, then apparently this Court's doors are open to conduct the credibility determination anew. Alas, "every end is instead a new beginning" for a majority of this Court. I cannot go along with that sort of sandbagging of state courts. New evidence should not justify the re-litigation of *Batson* claims. . . .

Page 1221. Place this material at the end of note 3.

See also People v. Gutierrez, 395 P.3d 186 (Cal. 2017) (prosecutor used 10 of 16 available challenges to remove Hispanic jurors, but trial judge concluded that those removals were based on nonracial grounds; California Supreme Court ruled that the record did not adequately support judge's finding as to one juror, and appellate courts on review should engage in comparative juror analysis); Johnson v. Commonwealth, 450 S.W.3d 696 (Ky. 2014) (prosecutor's explanation that he struck potential juror because he had gone to high school with her and had "personal knowledge" about her was not specific enough to satisfy *Batson*).

Page 1225. Place this material at the end of note 4.

See also Williams v. Pennsylvania, 579 U.S. __ (2016) (recusal was constitutionally required of state Supreme Court justice who served earlier as the district attorney who gave his official approval to seek the death penalty in the prisoner's case; recusal required when the likelihood of bias on the part of the judge "is too high to be constitutionally tolerable").

C. *Jury Deliberations and Verdicts*

Page 1225. Place this material at the end of the introductory paragraph.

Miguel Peña-Rodriguez v. Colorado
137 S. Ct. 855 (2017)

KENNEDY, J.*

The jury is a central foundation of our justice system and our democracy. Whatever its imperfections in a particular case, the jury is a necessary check on governmental power. The jury, over the centuries, has been an inspired, trusted, and effective instrument for resolving factual disputes and determining ultimate questions of guilt or innocence in criminal cases. Over the long course its judgments find acceptance in the community, an acceptance essential to respect for the rule of law. The jury is a tangible implementation of the principle that the law comes from the people.

In the era of our Nation's founding, the right to a jury trial already had existed and evolved for centuries, through and alongside the common law. The jury was considered a fundamental safeguard of individual liberty. See The Federalist No. 83, p. 451 (B. Warner ed. 1818) (A. Hamilton). The right to a jury trial in criminal cases was part of the Constitution as first drawn, and it was restated in the Sixth Amendment. . . .

Like all human institutions, the jury system has its flaws, yet experience shows that fair and impartial verdicts can be reached if the jury follows the court's instructions and undertakes deliberations that are honest, candid, robust, and based on common sense. A general rule has evolved to give substantial protection to verdict finality and to assure jurors that, once their verdict has been entered, it will not later be called into question based on the comments or conclusions they expressed during deliberations. This principle, itself centuries old, is often referred to as the no-impeachment rule. The instant case presents the question whether there is an exception to the no-impeachment rule when, after the jury is discharged, a juror comes forward with compelling evidence that

* [Justices Ginsburg, Breyer, Sotomayor, and Kagan joined this opinion.—EDS.]

another juror made clear and explicit statements indicating that racial animus was a significant motivating factor in his or her vote to convict.

I.

State prosecutors in Colorado brought criminal charges against petitioner, Miguel Angel Peña-Rodriguez, based on the following allegations. In 2007, in the bathroom of a Colorado horse-racing facility, a man sexually assaulted two teenage sisters. The girls told their father and identified the man as an employee of the racetrack. The police located and arrested petitioner. Each girl separately identified petitioner as the man who had assaulted her.

The State charged petitioner with harassment, unlawful sexual contact, and attempted sexual assault on a child. Before the jury was empaneled, members of the venire were repeatedly asked whether they believed that they could be fair and impartial in the case. A written questionnaire asked if there was "anything about you that you feel would make it difficult for you to be a fair juror." The court repeated the question to the panel of prospective jurors and encouraged jurors to speak in private with the court if they had any concerns about their impartiality. Defense counsel likewise asked whether anyone felt that "this is simply not a good case" for them to be a fair juror. None of the empaneled jurors expressed any reservations based on racial or any other bias. And none asked to speak with the trial judge.

After a 3-day trial, the jury found petitioner guilty of unlawful sexual contact and harassment, but it failed to reach a verdict on the attempted sexual assault charge. When the jury was discharged, the court gave them this instruction, as mandated by Colorado law:

> The question may arise whether you may now discuss this case with the lawyers, defendant, or other persons. For your guidance the court instructs you that whether you talk to anyone is entirely your own decision. . . . If any person persists in discussing the case over your objection, or becomes critical of your service either before or after any discussion has begun, please report it to me.

Following the discharge of the jury, petitioner's counsel entered the jury room to discuss the trial with the jurors. As the room was emptying, two jurors remained to speak with counsel in private. They stated that, during deliberations, another juror had expressed anti-Hispanic bias toward petitioner and petitioner's alibi witness. Petitioner's counsel reported this to the court and, with the court's supervision, obtained sworn affidavits from the two jurors.

The affidavits by the two jurors described a number of biased statements made by another juror, identified as Juror H.C. According to the two jurors, H.C. told the other jurors that he "believed the defendant was guilty because, in [H.C.'s] experience as an ex-law enforcement officer, Mexican men had a bravado that caused them to believe they could do whatever they wanted with women." The jurors reported that H.C. stated his belief that Mexican men are physically controlling of women because of their sense of entitlement, and further stated, "I think he did it because he's Mexican and Mexican men take whatever they want." According to the jurors, H.C. further explained that, in his experience, "nine times out of ten Mexican men were guilty of being aggressive toward women and young girls." Finally, the jurors recounted that Juror H.C. said that he did not find petitioner's alibi witness credible because, among other things, the witness was "an illegal." (In fact, the witness testified during trial that he was a legal resident of the United States.)

After reviewing the affidavits, the trial court acknowledged H.C.'s apparent bias. But the court denied petitioner's motion for a new trial, noting that the "actual deliberations that occur among the jurors are protected from inquiry under [Colorado Rule of Evidence] 606(b)." Like its federal counterpart, Colorado's Rule 606(b) generally prohibits a juror from testifying as to any statement made during deliberations in a proceeding inquiring into the validity of the verdict. The Colorado Rule reads as follows:

> (b) *Inquiry into validity of verdict or indictment*. Upon an inquiry into the validity of a verdict or indictment, a juror may not testify as to any matter or statement occurring during the course of the jury's deliberations or to the effect of anything upon his or any other juror's mind or emotions as influencing him to assent to or dissent from the verdict or indictment or concerning his mental processes in connection therewith. But a juror may testify about (1) whether extraneous prejudicial information was improperly brought to the jurors' attention, (2) whether any outside influence was improperly brought to bear upon any juror, or (3) whether there was a mistake in entering the verdict onto the verdict form. A juror's affidavit or evidence of any statement by the juror may not be received on a matter about which the juror would be precluded from testifying.

The verdict deemed final, petitioner was sentenced to two years' probation and was required to register as a sex offender. . . .

The Colorado Supreme Court affirmed by a vote of 4 to 3. The prevailing opinion relied on two decisions of this Court rejecting constitutional challenges to the federal no-impeachment rule as applied to evidence of juror misconduct or bias. See Tanner v. United States, 483 U.S. 107 (1987); Warger v. Shauers, 574 U.S. __ (2014). After reviewing those precedents, the court could find no "dividing line between different types of juror bias or misconduct," and thus no basis for permitting impeachment of the verdicts in petitioner's trial, notwithstanding H.C.'s apparent racial bias. This Court granted certiorari to decide whether there is a constitutional exception to the no-impeachment rule for instances of racial [or ethnic] bias. . . .

II.

A.

At common law jurors were forbidden to impeach their verdict, either by affidavit or live testimony. This rule originated in Vaise v. Delaval, 1 T.R. 11, 99 Eng. Rep. 944 (K.B. 1785). There, Lord Mansfield excluded juror testimony that the jury had decided the case through a game of chance. The Mansfield rule, as it came to be known, prohibited jurors, after the verdict was entered, from testifying either about their subjective mental processes or about objective events that occurred during deliberations.

American courts adopted the Mansfield rule as a matter of common law, though not in every detail. Some jurisdictions adopted a different, more flexible version of the no-impeachment bar known as the "Iowa rule." Under that rule, jurors were prevented only from testifying about their own subjective beliefs, thoughts, or motives during deliberations. See Wright v. Illinois & Miss. Tel. Co., 20 Iowa 195 (1866). Jurors could, however, testify about objective facts and events occurring during deliberations, in part because other jurors could corroborate that testimony.

An alternative approach, later referred to as the federal approach, stayed closer to the original Mansfield rule. Under this version of the rule, the no-impeachment bar permitted an exception only for testimony about events extraneous to the deliberative process, such as reliance on outside evidence—newspapers, dictionaries, and the like—or personal investigation of the facts.

This Court's early decisions did not establish a clear preference for a particular version of the no-impeachment rule. In United States v. Reid, 12 How. 361 (1852), the Court appeared open to the admission of juror testimony that the jurors had consulted newspapers during deliberations, but in the end it barred the evidence because the newspapers "had not the slightest influence" on the verdict. The *Reid* Court warned that juror testimony "ought always to be received with great caution." Yet it added an important admonition: "cases might arise in which it would be impossible to refuse" juror testimony "without violating the plainest principles of justice." . . .

Later, however, the Court rejected the more lenient Iowa rule. In McDonald v. Pless, 238 U.S. 264 (1915), the Court affirmed the exclusion of juror testimony about objective events in the jury room. There, the jury allegedly had calculated a damages award by averaging the numerical submissions of each member. As the Court explained, admitting that evidence would have "dangerous consequences": "no verdict would be safe" and the practice would "open the door to the most pernicious arts and tampering with jurors." Yet the Court reiterated its admonition from *Reid*, again cautioning that the no-impeachment rule might recognize exceptions "in the gravest and most important cases" where exclusion of juror affidavits might well violate "the plainest principles of justice."

The common-law development of the no-impeachment rule reached a milestone in 1975, when Congress adopted the Federal Rules of Evidence, including Rule 606(b). Congress, like the *McDonald* Court, rejected the Iowa rule. Instead it endorsed a broad no-impeachment rule, with only limited exceptions.

The version of the rule that Congress adopted was "no accident." The Advisory Committee at first drafted a rule reflecting the Iowa approach, prohibiting admission of juror testimony only as it related to jurors' mental processes in reaching a verdict. The Department of Justice, however, expressed concern over the preliminary rule. The Advisory Committee then drafted the more stringent version now in effect, prohibiting all juror testimony, with exceptions only where the jury had considered prejudicial extraneous evidence or was subject to other outside influence. Rules of Evidence for United States Courts and Magistrates, 56 F.R.D. 183, 265 (1972). The Court adopted this second version and transmitted it to Congress. . . . Congress enacted, and the President signed the Court's proposed rule. The substance of the Rule has not changed since 1975, except for a 2006 modification permitting evidence of a clerical mistake on the verdict form. . . .

This version of the no-impeachment rule has substantial merit. It promotes full and vigorous discussion by providing jurors with considerable assurance that after being discharged they will not be summoned to recount their deliberations, and they will not otherwise be harassed or annoyed by litigants seeking to challenge the verdict. The rule gives stability and finality to verdicts.

B.

Some version of the no-impeachment rule is followed in every State and the District of Columbia. Variations make classification imprecise, but, as a general matter, it appears that 42 jurisdictions follow the Federal Rule, while 9 follow the Iowa Rule. Within both classifications there is a diversity of approaches. Nine jurisdictions that follow the Federal Rule have codified exceptions other than those listed in Federal Rule 606(b). At least 16 jurisdictions, 11 of which follow the Federal Rule, have recognized an exception to the no-impeachment bar under the circumstances the Court faces here: juror testimony that racial bias played a part in deliberations. According to the parties and amici, only one State other than Colorado has addressed this issue and declined to recognize an exception for racial bias. See Commonwealth v. Steele, 961 A.2d 786 (Penn. 2008). . . .

C.

In addressing the scope of the common-law no-impeachment rule before Rule 606(b)'s adoption, the *Reid* and *McDonald* Courts noted the possibility of an exception to the rule in the "gravest and most important cases." Yet since the enactment of Rule 606(b), the Court has addressed the precise question whether the Constitution mandates an exception to it in just two instances.

In its first case, Tanner v. United States, 483 U.S. 107 (1987), the Court rejected a Sixth Amendment exception for evidence that some jurors were under the influence of drugs and alcohol during the trial. Central to the Court's reasoning were the "long-recognized and very substantial concerns" supporting "the protection of jury deliberations from intrusive inquiry." The *Tanner* Court echoed *McDonald*'s concern that, if attorneys could use juror testimony to attack verdicts, jurors would be "harassed and beset by the defeated party," thus destroying "all frankness and freedom of discussion and conference." The Court was concerned, moreover, that attempts to impeach a verdict would "disrupt the finality of the process" and undermine both "jurors' willingness to return an unpopular verdict" and "the community's trust in a system that relies on the decisions of laypeople."

The *Tanner* Court outlined existing, significant safeguards for the defendant's right to an impartial and competent jury beyond post-trial juror testimony. At the outset of the trial process, voir dire provides an opportunity for the court and counsel to examine members of the venire for impartiality. As a trial proceeds, the court, counsel, and court personnel have some opportunity to learn of any juror misconduct. And, before the verdict, jurors themselves can report misconduct to the court. These procedures do not undermine the stability of a verdict once rendered. Even after the trial, evidence of misconduct other than juror testimony can be used to attempt to impeach the verdict. Balancing these interests and safeguards against the defendant's Sixth Amendment interest in that case, the Court affirmed the exclusion of affidavits pertaining to the jury's inebriated state.

The second case to consider the general issue presented here was Warger v. Shauers, 135 S. Ct. 521 (2014). The Court again rejected the argument that, in the circumstances there, the jury trial right required an exception to the no-impeachment rule. *Warger* involved a civil case where, after the verdict was entered, the losing party sought to proffer evidence that the jury forewoman had failed to disclose prodefendant bias during voir dire. As in *Tanner*, the Court put substantial reliance on existing safeguards for a fair trial. The Court stated: "Even if jurors lie in voir dire in a way that conceals bias, juror impartiality is adequately assured by the parties' ability to bring to the court's attention any evidence of bias before the verdict is rendered, and to employ nonjuror evidence even after the verdict is rendered."

In *Warger*, however, the Court did reiterate that the no-impeachment rule may admit exceptions. As in *Reid* and *McDonald*, the Court warned of "juror bias so extreme that, almost by definition, the jury trial right has been abridged." "If and when such a case arises," the Court indicated it would "consider whether the usual safeguards are or are not sufficient to protect the integrity of the process."

The recognition in *Warger* that there may be extreme cases where the jury trial right requires an exception to the no-impeachment rule must be interpreted in context as a guarded, cautious statement. This caution is warranted to avoid formulating an exception that might undermine the jury dynamics and finality interests the no-impeachment rule seeks to protect. Today, however, the Court faces the question that *Reid*, *McDonald*, and *Warger* left open. The Court must decide whether the Constitution requires an exception to the no-impeachment rule when a juror's statements indicate that racial animus was a significant motivating factor in his or her finding of guilt.

III.

It must become the heritage of our Nation to rise above racial classifications that are so inconsistent with our commitment to the equal dignity of all persons. This imperative to purge racial prejudice from the administration of justice was given new force and direction by the ratification of the Civil War Amendments.

"[The] central purpose of the Fourteenth Amendment was to eliminate racial discrimination emanating from official sources in the States." McLaughlin v. Florida, 379 U.S. 184 (1964). In the years before and after the ratification of the Fourteenth Amendment, it became clear that racial discrimination in the jury system posed a particular threat both to the promise of the Amendment and to the integrity of the jury trial. "Almost immediately after the Civil War, the South began a practice that would continue for many decades: All-white juries punished black defendants particularly harshly, while simultaneously refusing to punish violence by whites, including Ku Klux Klan members, against blacks and Republicans." Forman, Juries and Race in the Nineteenth Century, 113 Yale L.J. 895 (2004). To take one example, just in the years 1865 and 1866, all-white juries in Texas decided a total of 500 prosecutions of white defendants charged with killing African-Americans. All 500 were acquitted. The stark and unapologetic nature of race-motivated outcomes challenged the American belief that "the jury was a bulwark of liberty," and prompted Congress to pass legislation to integrate the jury system and to bar persons from eligibility for jury service if they had conspired to deny the civil rights of African-Americans. Members of Congress stressed that the legislation was necessary to preserve the right to a fair trial and to guarantee the equal protection of the laws.

The duty to confront racial animus in the justice system is not the legislature's alone. Time and again, this Court has been called upon to enforce the Constitution's guarantee against state-sponsored racial discrimination in the jury system. Beginning in 1880, the Court interpreted the Fourteenth Amendment to prohibit the exclusion of jurors on the basis of race. Strauder v. West Virginia, 100 U.S. 303 (1880). The Court has repeatedly struck down laws and practices that systematically exclude racial minorities from juries. See, e.g., Neal v. Delaware, 103 U.S. 370 (1881); Hollins v. Oklahoma, 295 U.S. 394 (1935) (per curiam); Avery v. Georgia, 345 U.S. 559 (1953); Hernandez v. Texas, 347 U.S. 475 (1954); Castaneda v. Partida, 430 U.S. 482 (1977). To guard against discrimination in jury selection, the Court has ruled that no litigant may exclude a prospective juror on the basis of race. Batson v. Kentucky, 476 U.S. 79 (1986); Edmonson v. Leesville Concrete Co., 500 U.S. 614 (1991); Georgia v. McCollum, 505 U.S. 42 (1992). In an effort to ensure that individuals who sit on juries are free of racial bias, the Court has held that the Constitution at times demands that defendants be permitted to ask questions about racial bias during voir dire. Ham v. South Carolina, 409 U.S. 524 (1973); Turner v. Murray, 476 U.S. 28 (1986).

The unmistakable principle underlying these precedents is that discrimination on the basis of race, "odious in all aspects, is especially pernicious in the administration of justice." Rose v. Mitchell, 443 U.S. 545 (1979). The jury is to be "a criminal defendant's fundamental protection of life and liberty against race or color prejudice." McCleskey v. Kemp, 481 U.S. 279 (1987). Permitting racial prejudice in the jury system damages "both the fact and the perception" of the jury's role as "a vital check against the wrongful exercise of power by the State."

IV.

This case lies at the intersection of the Court's decisions endorsing the no-impeachment rule and its decisions seeking to eliminate racial bias in the jury system. The two lines of precedent, however, need not conflict.

Racial bias of the kind alleged in this case differs in critical ways from the compromise verdict in *McDonald*, the drug and alcohol abuse in *Tanner*, or the pro-defendant bias in *Warger*. The behavior in those cases is troubling and unacceptable, but each involved anomalous behavior from a single jury—or juror—gone off course. Jurors are presumed to follow their oath, and neither history nor common experience show that the jury system is rife with mischief of these or similar kinds. To attempt to rid the jury of every irregularity of this sort would be to expose it to unrelenting scrutiny. "It is not at all clear . . . that the jury system could survive such efforts to perfect it."

The same cannot be said about racial bias, a familiar and recurring evil that, if left unaddressed, would risk systemic injury to the administration of justice. This Court's decisions demonstrate that racial bias implicates unique historical, constitutional, and institutional concerns. An effort to address the most grave and serious statements of racial bias is not an effort to perfect the jury but to ensure that our legal system remains capable of coming ever closer to the promise of equal treatment under the law that is so central to a functioning democracy.

Racial bias is distinct in a pragmatic sense as well. In past cases this Court has relied on other safeguards to protect the right to an impartial jury. Some of those safeguards, to be sure, can disclose racial bias. Voir dire at the outset of trial, observation of juror demeanor and conduct during trial, juror reports before the verdict, and nonjuror evidence after trial are important mechanisms for discovering bias. Yet their operation may be compromised, or they may prove insufficient. For instance, this Court has noted the dilemma faced by trial court judges and counsel in deciding whether to explore potential racial bias at voir dire. Generic questions about juror impartiality may not expose specific attitudes or biases that can poison jury deliberations. Yet more pointed questions "could well exacerbate whatever prejudice might exist without substantially aiding in exposing it."

The stigma that attends racial bias may make it difficult for a juror to report inappropriate statements during the course of juror deliberations. It is one thing to accuse a fellow juror of having a personal experience that improperly influences her consideration of the case, as would have been required in *Warger*. It is quite another to call her a bigot.

The recognition that certain of the *Tanner* safeguards may be less effective in rooting out racial bias than other kinds of bias is not dispositive. All forms of improper bias pose challenges to the trial process. But there is a sound basis to treat racial bias with added precaution. A constitutional rule that racial bias in the justice system must be addressed—including, in some instances, after the verdict has been entered—is necessary to prevent a systemic loss of confidence in jury verdicts, a confidence that is a central premise of the Sixth Amendment trial right.

B.

For the reasons explained above, the Court now holds that where a juror makes a clear statement that indicates he or she relied on racial stereotypes or animus to convict a criminal defendant, the Sixth Amendment requires that the no-impeachment rule give way in order to permit the trial court to consider the evidence of the juror's statement and any resulting denial of the jury trial guarantee.

Not every offhand comment indicating racial bias or hostility will justify setting aside the no-impeachment bar to allow further judicial inquiry. For the inquiry to proceed, there must be a showing that one or more jurors made statements exhibiting overt racial bias that cast serious doubt on the fairness and impartiality of the jury's deliberations and resulting verdict. To qualify, the statement must tend to show that racial animus was a significant motivating factor in the juror's vote to convict. Whether that threshold showing has been satisfied is a matter committed to the substantial discretion of the trial court in light of all the circumstances, including the content and timing of the alleged statements and the reliability of the proffered evidence.

The practical mechanics of acquiring and presenting such evidence will no doubt be shaped and guided by state rules of professional ethics and local court rules, both of which often limit counsel's post-trial contact with jurors. These limits seek to provide jurors some protection when they return to their daily affairs after the verdict has been entered. But while a juror can always tell counsel they do not wish to discuss the case, jurors in some instances may come forward of their own accord.

That is what happened here. In this case the alleged statements by a juror were egregious and unmistakable in their reliance on racial bias. Not only did juror H.C. deploy a dangerous racial stereotype to conclude petitioner was guilty and his alibi witness should not be believed, but he also encouraged other jurors to join him in convicting on that basis.

Petitioner's counsel did not seek out the two jurors' allegations of racial bias. Pursuant to Colorado's mandatory jury instruction, the trial court had set limits on juror contact and encouraged jurors to inform the court if anyone harassed them about their role in the case. Similar limits on juror contact can be found in other jurisdictions that recognize a racial-bias exception. See, e.g., Fla. Standard Jury Instrs. in Crim. Cases No. 4.2 ("Although you are at liberty to speak with anyone about your deliberations, you are also at liberty to refuse to speak to anyone"); Mass. Office of Jury Comm'r, Trial Juror's Handbook ("You are not required to speak with anyone once the trial is over. . . . If anyone tries to learn this confidential information from you, or if you feel harassed or embarrassed in any way, you should report it to the court . . . immediately"); N.J. Crim. Model Jury Charges, Non 2C Charges, Dismissal of Jury ("It will be up to each of you to decide whether to speak about your service as a juror").

With the understanding that they were under no obligation to speak out, the jurors approached petitioner's counsel, within a short time after the verdict, to relay their concerns about H.C.'s statements. A similar pattern is common in cases involving juror allegations of racial bias. Pursuant to local court rules, petitioner's counsel then sought and received permission from the court to contact the two jurors and obtain affidavits limited to recounting the exact statements made by H.C. that exhibited racial bias.

While the trial court concluded that Colorado's Rule 606(b) did not permit it even to consider the resulting affidavits, the Court's holding today removes that bar. When jurors disclose an instance of racial bias as serious as the one involved in this case, the law must not wholly disregard its occurrence.

C.

As the preceding discussion makes clear, the Court relies on the experiences of the 17 jurisdictions that have recognized a racial-bias exception to the no-impeachment rule—some for over half a century—with no signs of an increase in juror harassment or a loss of juror willingness to engage in searching and candid deliberations.

The experience of these jurisdictions, and the experience of the courts going forward, will inform the proper exercise of trial judge discretion in these and related matters. This case does not ask, and the Court need not address, what procedures a trial court must follow when confronted with a motion for a new trial based on juror testimony of racial bias. The Court also does not decide the appropriate standard for determining when evidence of racial bias is sufficient to require that the verdict be set aside and a new trial be granted.

D.

It is proper to observe as well that there are standard and existing processes designed to prevent racial bias in jury deliberations. The advantages of careful voir dire have already been noted. And other safeguards deserve mention.

Trial courts, often at the outset of the case and again in their final jury instructions, explain the jurors' duty to review the evidence and reach a verdict in a fair and impartial way, free from bias of any kind. Some instructions are framed by trial judges based on their own learning and experience. . . . Instructions may emphasize the group dynamic of deliberations by urging jurors to share their questions and conclusions with their colleagues. Probing and thoughtful deliberation improves the likelihood that other jurors can confront the flawed nature of reasoning that is prompted or influenced by improper biases, whether racial or otherwise. These dynamics can help ensure that the exception is limited to rare cases. . . .

The Nation must continue to make strides to overcome race-based discrimination. The progress that has already been made underlies the Court's insistence that blatant racial prejudice is antithetical to the functioning of the jury system and must be confronted in egregious cases like this one despite the general bar of the no-impeachment rule. It is the mark of a maturing legal system that it seeks to understand and to implement the lessons of history. The Court now seeks to strengthen the broader principle that society can and must move forward by achieving the thoughtful, rational dialogue at the foundation of both the jury system and the free society that sustains our Constitution. . . .

THOMAS, J., dissenting.

. . . The Court today acknowledges that the States "adopted the Mansfield rule as a matter of common law," but ascribes no significance to that fact. I would hold that it is dispositive. Our common-law history does not establish that—in either 1791 (when the Sixth Amendment was ratified) or 1868 (when the Fourteenth Amendment was ratified)—a defendant had the right to impeach a verdict with juror testimony of juror misconduct. In fact, it strongly suggests that such evidence was prohibited. In the absence of a definitive common-law tradition permitting impeachment by juror testimony, we have no basis to invoke a constitutional provision that merely follows out "the established course of the common law in all trials for crimes," 3 J. Story, Commentaries on the Constitution of the United States § 1785, at 662, to overturn Colorado's decision to preserve the no-impeachment rule.

Perhaps good reasons exist to curtail or abandon the no-impeachment rule. Some States have done so, and others have not. Ultimately, that question is not for us to decide. It should be left to the political process. . . . In its attempt to stimulate a "thoughtful, rational dialogue" on race relations, the Court today ends the political process and imposes a uniform, national rule. The Constitution does not require such a rule. Neither should we.

ALITO, J., dissenting.*

Our legal system has many rules that restrict the admission of evidence of statements made under circumstances in which confidentiality is thought to be essential. Statements made to an attorney in obtaining legal advice, statements to a treating physician, and statements made to a spouse or member of the clergy are familiar examples. Even if a criminal defendant whose constitutional rights are at stake has a critical need to obtain and introduce evidence of such statements, long-established rules stand in the way. The goal of avoiding interference with confidential communications of great value has long been thought to justify the loss of important evidence and the effect on our justice system that this loss entails.

The present case concerns a rule like those just mentioned, namely, the age-old rule against attempting to overturn or "impeach" a jury's verdict by offering statements made by jurors during the course of deliberations. For centuries, it has been the judgment of experienced judges, trial attorneys, scholars, and lawmakers that allowing jurors to testify after a trial about what took place in the jury room would undermine the system of trial by jury that is integral to our legal system.

Juries occupy a unique place in our justice system. The other participants in a trial—the presiding judge, the attorneys, the witnesses—function in an arena governed by strict rules of law. Their every word is recorded and may be closely scrutinized for missteps.

When jurors retire to deliberate, however, they enter a space that is not regulated in the same way. Jurors are ordinary people. They are expected to speak, debate, argue, and make decisions the way ordinary people do in their daily lives. Our Constitution places great value on this way of thinking, speaking, and deciding. The jury trial right protects parties in court cases from being judged by a special class of trained

---

* [Chief Justice Roberts and Justice Thomas joined this opinion—EDS.]

professionals who do not speak the language of ordinary people and may not understand or appreciate the way ordinary people live their lives. To protect that right, the door to the jury room has been locked, and the confidentiality of jury deliberations has been closely guarded.

Today, with the admirable intention of providing justice for one criminal defendant, the Court not only pries open the door; it rules that respecting the privacy of the jury room, as our legal system has done for centuries, violates the Constitution. This is a startling development, and although the Court tries to limit the degree of intrusion, it is doubtful that there are principled grounds for preventing the expansion of today's holding.

The Court justifies its decision on the ground that the nature of the confidential communication at issue in this particular case—a clear expression of what the Court terms racial bias—is uniquely harmful to our criminal justice system. And the Court is surely correct that even a tincture of racial bias can inflict great damage on that system, which is dependent on the public's trust. But until today, the argument that the Court now finds convincing has not been thought to be sufficient to overcome confidentiality rules like the one at issue here.

Suppose that a prosecution witness gives devastating but false testimony against a defendant, and suppose that the witness's motivation is racial bias. Suppose that the witness admits this to his attorney, his spouse, and a member of the clergy. Suppose that the defendant, threatened with conviction for a serious crime and a lengthy term of imprisonment, seeks to compel the attorney, the spouse, or the member of the clergy to testify about the witness's admissions. Even though the constitutional rights of the defendant hang in the balance, the defendant's efforts to obtain the testimony would fail. The Court provides no good reason why the result in this case should not be the same.

Today's decision—especially if it is expanded in the ways that seem likely—will invite the harms that no-impeachment rules were designed to prevent.

First, as the Court explained in *Tanner*, "postverdict scrutiny of juror conduct" will inhibit "full and frank discussion in the jury room." Or, as the Senate Report put it: "[Common] fairness requires that absolute privacy be preserved for jurors to engage in the full and free debate necessary to the attainment of just verdicts. Jurors will not be able to function effectively if their deliberations are to be scrutinized in post-trial litigation."

Today's ruling will also prompt losing parties and their friends, supporters, and attorneys to contact and seek to question jurors, and this pestering may erode citizens' willingness to serve on juries. Many jurisdictions now have rules that prohibit or restrict post-verdict contact with jurors, but whether those rules will survive today's decision is an open question—as is the effect of this decision on privilege rules such as those noted at the outset of this opinion.

Where post-verdict approaches are permitted or occur, there is almost certain to be an increase in harassment, arm-twisting, and outright coercion. As one treatise explains, "[a] juror who reluctantly joined a verdict is likely to be sympathetic to overtures by the loser, and persuadable to the view that his own consent rested on false or impermissible considerations, and the truth will be hard to know." 3 C. Mueller & L. Kirkpatrick, Federal Evidence § 6:16, p. 75 (4th ed. 2013). . . .

The Court's only response is that some jurisdictions already make an exception for racial bias, and the Court detects no signs of "a loss of juror willingness to engage in searching and candid deliberations." One wonders what sort of outward signs the Court would expect to see if jurors in these jurisdictions do not speak as freely in the jury room as their counterparts in jurisdictions with strict no-impeachment rules. Gathering and assessing evidence regarding the quality of jury deliberations in different jurisdictions would be a daunting enterprise, and the Court offers no indication that anybody has undertaken that task.

In short, the majority barely bothers to engage with the policy issues implicated by no-impeachment rules. But even if it had carefully grappled with those issues, it still would have no basis for exalting its own judgment over that of the many expert policymakers who have endorsed broad no-impeachment rule.

The Court's decision is well-intentioned. It seeks to remedy a flaw in the jury trial system, but as this Court said some years ago, it is questionable whether our system of trial by jury can endure this attempt to perfect it. . . .

D. The Public as Decisionmaker

1. Public Access to Trials

Page 1252. Place this material at the end of note 3.

Weaver v. Massachusetts, 137 S. Ct. 1899 (2017) (jury voir dire must be public unless judge gives appropriate reason for closing courtroom); Commonwealth v. Fujita, 23 N.E.3d 882 (Mass. 2015) (based on common-law right of public access to judicial records, names of jurors must be made public after trial ends unless trial judge can point to reason for confidentiality beyond juror preference).

Chapter 18

Witnesses and Proof

A. *Burden of Proof*

1. Reasonable Doubt

Page 1270. Place this material at the end of note 1.

See also Commonwealth v. Russell, 23 N.E.3d 867 (Mass. 2015) (updating state jury instruction to clarify "moral certainty" phrase to mean "the highest degree of certainty possible in matters relating to human affairs—based solely on the evidence that has been put before you in this case.").

Page 1271. Place this material at the end of note 2.

See also Michael D. Cicchini & Lawrence T. White, Testing the Impact of Criminal Jury Instructions on Verdicts: A Conceptual Replication, 117 Colum. L. Rev. Online No. 2 (2017) (experiment finding statistically significant difference in conviction rates between mock jurors who were properly instructed on reasonable doubt, and mock jurors who were instead instructed "to search for the truth," with latter group nearly twice as likely to mistakenly believe they could convict defendant even if they had a reasonable doubt about guilt).

B. Confrontation of Witnesses

2. Out-of-Court Statements by Unavailable Witnesses

Page 1302. Place this material before the Notes.

Ohio v. Darius Clark
135 S. Ct. 2173 (2015)

ALITO, J.*

Darius Clark sent his girlfriend hundreds of miles away to engage in prostitution and agreed to care for her two young children while she was out of town. A day later, teachers discovered red marks on her 3-year-old son, and the boy identified Clark as his abuser. The question in this case is whether the Sixth Amendment's Confrontation Clause prohibited prosecutors from introducing those statements when the child was not available to be cross-examined. Because neither the child nor his teachers had the primary purpose of assisting in Clark's prosecution, the child's statements do not implicate the Confrontation Clause and therefore were admissible at trial.

Darius Clark, who went by the nickname "Dee," lived in Cleveland, Ohio, with his girlfriend, T.T., and her two children: L.P., a 3-year-old boy, and A.T., an 18-month-old girl. Clark was also T.T.'s pimp, and he would regularly send her on trips to Washington, D.C., to work as a prostitute. In March 2010, T.T. went on one such trip, and she left the children in Clark's care.

The next day, Clark took L.P. to preschool. In the lunchroom, one of L.P.'s teachers, Ramona Whitley, observed that L.P.'s left eye appeared bloodshot. She asked him "what happened," and he initially said nothing. Eventually, however, he told the teacher that he "fell." When they moved into the brighter lights of a classroom, Whitley noticed "red marks, like whips of some sort," on L.P.'s face. She notified the lead teacher, Debra

* [Chief Justice Roberts and Justices Kennedy, Breyer, Sotomayor, and Kagan joined this opinion.—EDS.]

Jones, who asked L.P., "Who did this? What happened to you?" According to Jones, L.P. "seemed kind of bewildered" and "said something like, Dee, Dee." Jones asked L.P. whether Dee is "big or little," to which L.P. responded that "Dee is big." Jones then brought L.P. to her supervisor, who lifted the boy's shirt, revealing more injuries. Whitley called a child abuse hotline to alert authorities about the suspected abuse.

When Clark later arrived at the school, he denied responsibility for the injuries and quickly left with L.P. The next day, a social worker found the children at Clark's mother's house and took them to a hospital, where a physician discovered additional injuries suggesting child abuse. L.P. had a black eye, belt marks on his back and stomach, and bruises all over his body. A.T. had two black eyes, a swollen hand, and a large burn on her cheek, and two pigtails had been ripped out at the roots of her hair.

A grand jury indicted Clark on five counts of felonious assault (four related to A.T. and one related to L.P.), two counts of endangering children (one for each child), and two counts of domestic violence (one for each child). At trial, the State introduced L.P.'s statements to his teachers as evidence of Clark's guilt, but L.P. did not testify. Under Ohio law, children younger than 10 years old are incompetent to testify if they "appear incapable of receiving just impressions of the facts and transactions respecting which they are examined, or of relating them truly." Ohio Rule Evid. 601(A). After conducting a hearing, the trial court concluded that L.P. was not competent to testify. But under Ohio Rule of Evidence 807, which allows the admission of reliable hearsay by child abuse victims, the court ruled that L.P.'s statements to his teachers bore sufficient guarantees of trustworthiness to be admitted as evidence.

Clark moved to exclude testimony about L.P.'s out-of-court statements under the Confrontation Clause. The trial court denied the motion, ruling that L.P.'s responses were not testimonial statements covered by the Sixth Amendment. The jury found Clark guilty on all counts except for one assault count related to A.T., and it sentenced him to 28 years' imprisonment. Clark appealed his conviction, and a state appellate court reversed on the ground that the introduction of L.P.'s out-of-court statements violated the Confrontation Clause.

In a 4-to-3 decision, the Supreme Court of Ohio affirmed. It held that, under this Court's Confrontation Clause decisions, L.P.'s statements qualified as testimonial because the primary purpose of the teachers' questioning "was not to deal with an existing emergency but rather to gather evidence potentially relevant to a subsequent criminal prosecution." The court noted that Ohio has a "mandatory reporting" law that requires certain professionals, including preschool teachers, to report suspected child abuse to government authorities. In the court's view, the teachers acted as agents of the State under the mandatory reporting law and "sought facts concerning past criminal activity to identify the person responsible, eliciting statements that are functionally identical to live, in-court testimony, doing precisely what a witness does on direct examination." . . .

The Sixth Amendment's Confrontation Clause, which is binding on the States through the Fourteenth Amendment, provides: "In all criminal prosecutions, the accused shall enjoy the right . . . to be confronted with the witnesses against him." In Ohio v. Roberts, 448 U.S. 56, 66 (1980), we interpreted the Clause to permit the admission of out-of-court statements by an unavailable witness, so long as the statements bore "adequate indicia of reliability." Such indicia are present, we held, if "the evidence falls within a firmly rooted hearsay exception" or bears "particularized guarantees of trustworthiness."

In Crawford v. Washington, 541 U.S. 36 (2004), we adopted a different approach. We explained that "witnesses," under the Confrontation Clause, are those "who bear testimony," and we defined "testimony" as "a solemn declaration or affirmation made for the purpose of establishing or proving some fact." The Sixth Amendment, we concluded, prohibits the introduction of testimonial statements by a nontestifying witness, unless the witness is "unavailable to testify, and the defendant had had a prior opportunity for cross-examination." Applying that definition to the facts in *Crawford,* we held that statements by a witness during police questioning at the station house were testimonial and thus could not be admitted. But our decision in *Crawford* did not offer an exhaustive definition of "testimonial" statements. Instead, *Crawford* stated that the label "applies at a minimum to prior testimony at a preliminary hearing, before a grand jury, or at a former trial; and to police interrogations."

Our more recent cases have labored to flesh out what it means for a statement to be "testimonial." In Davis v. Washington and Hammon v. Indiana, 547 U.S. 813 (2006), which we decided together, we dealt with statements given to law enforcement officers by the victims of domestic abuse. The victim in *Davis* made statements to a 911 emergency operator during and shortly after her boyfriend's violent attack. In *Hammon,* the victim, after being isolated from her abusive husband, made statements to police that were memorialized in a "battery affidavit."

We held that the statements in *Hammon* were testimonial, while the statements in *Davis* were not. Announcing what has come to be known as the "primary purpose" test, we explained: "Statements are nontestimonial when made in the course of police interrogation under circumstances objectively indicating that the primary purpose of the interrogation is to enable police assistance to meet an ongoing emergency. They are testimonial when the circumstances objectively indicate that there is no such ongoing emergency, and that the primary purpose of the interrogation is to establish or prove past events potentially relevant to later criminal prosecution." Because the cases involved statements to law enforcement officers, we reserved the question whether similar statements to individuals other than law enforcement officers would raise similar issues under the Confrontation Clause.

In Michigan v. Bryant, 562 U.S. 344 (2011), we further expounded on the primary purpose test. The inquiry, we emphasized, must consider "all of the relevant circumstances." And we reiterated our view in *Davis* that, when "the primary purpose of an interrogation is to respond to an ongoing emergency, its purpose is not to create a record for trial and thus is not within the scope of the Confrontation Clause." At the same time, we noted that "there may be *other* circumstances, aside from ongoing emergencies, when a statement is not procured with a primary purpose of creating an out-of-court substitute for trial testimony." "The existence *vel non* of an ongoing emergency is not the touchstone of the testimonial inquiry." Instead, "whether an ongoing emergency exists is simply one factor . . . that informs the ultimate inquiry regarding the 'primary purpose' of an interrogation."

One additional factor is "the informality of the situation and the interrogation." A "formal station-house interrogation," like the questioning in *Crawford,* is more likely to provoke testimonial statements, while less formal questioning is less likely to reflect a primary purpose aimed at obtaining testimonial evidence against the accused. And in determining whether a statement is testimonial, "standard rules of hearsay, designed to identify some statements as reliable, will be relevant." In the end, the question is whether, in light of all the circumstances, viewed objectively, the "primary purpose" of the conversation was to "create an out-of-court substitute for trial testimony." Applying these principles in *Bryant,* we held that the statements made by a dying victim about his assailant were not testimonial because the circumstances objectively indicated that the conversation was primarily aimed at quelling an ongoing emergency, not establishing evidence for the prosecution. Because the relevant statements were made to law enforcement officers, we again declined to decide whether the same analysis applies to statements made to individuals other than the police.

Thus, under our precedents, a statement cannot fall within the Confrontation Clause unless its primary purpose was testimonial. "Where no such primary purpose exists, the admissibility of a statement is the concern of state and federal rules of evidence, not the Confrontation Clause." But that does not mean that the Confrontation Clause bars every statement that satisfies the "primary purpose" test. We have recognized that the Confrontation Clause does not prohibit the introduction of out-of-court statements that would have been admissible in a criminal case at the time of the founding. See Giles v. California, 554 U.S. 353 (2008). Thus, the primary purpose test is a necessary, but not always sufficient, condition for the exclusion of out-of-court statements under the Confrontation Clause.

In this case, we consider statements made to preschool teachers, not the police. We are therefore presented with the question we have repeatedly reserved: whether statements to persons other than law enforcement officers are subject to the Confrontation Clause. Because at least some statements to individuals who are not law enforcement officers could conceivably raise confrontation concerns, we decline to adopt a categorical rule excluding them from the Sixth Amendment's reach. Nevertheless, such statements are much less likely to be testimonial than statements to law enforcement officers. And considering all the relevant circumstances here, L.P.'s statements clearly were not made with the primary purpose of creating evidence for Clark's prosecution. Thus, their introduction at trial did not violate the Confrontation Clause.

L.P.'s statements occurred in the context of an ongoing emergency involving suspected child abuse. When L.P.'s teachers noticed his injuries, they rightly became worried that the 3-year-old was the victim of serious violence. Because the teachers needed to know whether it was safe to release L.P. to his guardian at the end of the day, they needed to determine who might be abusing the child.[2] Thus, the immediate concern was to protect a vulnerable child who needed help. Our holding in *Bryant* is instructive. As in *Bryant,* the emergency in this case was ongoing, and the circumstances were not entirely clear. L.P.'s teachers were not sure who had abused him or how best to secure his safety. Nor were they sure whether any other children might be at risk. As a result, their questions and L.P.'s answers were primarily aimed at identifying and ending the threat. Though not as harried, the conversation here was also similar to the 911 call in *Davis*. The teachers' questions were meant to identify the abuser in order to protect the victim from future attacks. Whether the teachers thought that this would be done by apprehending the abuser or by some other means is irrelevant. And the circumstances in this case were unlike the interrogation in *Hammon,* where the police knew the identity of the assailant and questioned the victim after shielding her from potential harm.

There is no indication that the primary purpose of the conversation was to gather evidence for Clark's prosecution. On the contrary, it is clear that the first objective was to protect L.P. At no point did the teachers inform L.P. that his answers would be used to arrest or punish his abuser. L.P. never hinted that he intended his statements to be used by the police or prosecutors. And the conversation between L.P. and his teachers was informal and spontaneous. The teachers asked L.P. about his injuries immediately upon discovering them, in the informal setting of a preschool lunchroom and classroom, and they did so precisely as any concerned citizen would talk to a child who might be the victim of abuse. This was nothing like the formalized station-house questioning in *Crawford* or the police interrogation and battery affidavit in *Hammon*.

L.P.'s age fortifies our conclusion that the statements in question were not testimonial. Statements by very young children will rarely, if ever, implicate the Confrontation Clause. Few preschool students

---

[2] In fact, the teachers and a social worker who had come to the school *were* reluctant to release L.P. into Clark's care after the boy identified Clark as his abuser. But after a brief "stare-down" with the social worker, Clark bolted out the door with L.P., and social services were not able to locate the children until the next day.

understand the details of our criminal justice system. Rather, research on children's understanding of the legal system finds that young children "have little understanding of prosecution." Brief for American Professional Society on the Abuse of Children as *Amicus Curiae*. And Clark does not dispute those findings. Thus, it is extremely unlikely that a 3-year-old child in L.P.'s position would intend his statements to be a substitute for trial testimony. On the contrary, a young child in these circumstances would simply want the abuse to end, would want to protect other victims, or would have no discernible purpose at all.

As a historical matter, moreover, there is strong evidence that statements made in circumstances similar to those facing L.P. and his teachers were admissible at common law. See Lyon & LaMagna, The History of Children's Hearsay: From Old Bailey to Post-*Davis*, 82 Ind. L.J. 1029, 1030 (2007); J. Langbein, The Origins of Adversary Criminal Trial (2003) ("The Old Bailey" court in 18th-century London "tolerated flagrant hearsay in rape prosecutions involving a child victim who was not competent to testify because she was too young to appreciate the significance of her oath"). And when 18th-century courts excluded statements of this sort they appeared to do so because the child should have been ruled competent to testify, not because the statements were otherwise inadmissible. It is thus highly doubtful that statements like L.P.'s ever would have been understood to raise Confrontation Clause concerns. Neither *Crawford* nor any of the cases that it has produced has mounted evidence that the adoption of the Confrontation Clause was understood to require the exclusion of evidence that was regularly admitted in criminal cases at the time of the founding. Certainly, the statements in this case are nothing like the notorious use of *ex parte* examination in Sir Walter Raleigh's trial for treason, which we have frequently identified as "the principal evil at which the Confrontation Clause was directed."

Finally, although we decline to adopt a rule that statements to individuals who are not law enforcement officers are categorically outside the Sixth Amendment, the fact that L.P. was speaking to his teachers remains highly relevant. Courts must evaluate challenged statements in context, and part of that context is the questioner's identity. Statements made to someone who is not principally charged with uncovering and prosecuting criminal behavior are significantly less likely to be testimonial than statements given to law enforcement officers. It is common sense that the relationship between a student and his teacher is very different from that between a citizen and the police. We do not ignore that reality. In light of these circumstances, the Sixth Amendment did not prohibit the State from introducing L.P.'s statements at trial.

Clark's efforts to avoid this conclusion are all off-base. He emphasizes Ohio's mandatory reporting obligations, in an attempt to equate L.P.'s teachers with the police and their caring questions with official interrogations. But the comparison is inapt. The teachers' pressing concern was to protect L.P. and remove him from harm's way. Like all good teachers, they undoubtedly would have acted with the same purpose whether or not they had a state-law duty to report abuse. And mandatory reporting statutes alone cannot convert a conversation between a concerned teacher and her student into a law enforcement mission aimed primarily at gathering evidence for a prosecution.

It is irrelevant that the teachers' questions and their duty to report the matter had the natural tendency to result in Clark's prosecution. The statements at issue in *Davis* and *Bryant* supported the defendants' convictions, and the police always have an obligation to ask questions to resolve ongoing emergencies. Yet, we held in those cases that the Confrontation Clause did not prohibit introduction of the statements because they were not primarily intended to be testimonial. Thus, Clark is also wrong to suggest that admitting L.P.'s statements would be fundamentally unfair given that Ohio law does not allow incompetent children to testify. In any Confrontation Clause case, the individual who provided the out-of-court statement is not available as an in-court witness, but the testimony is admissible under an exception to the hearsay rules and is probative of the defendant's guilt. The fact that the witness is unavailable because of a different rule of evidence does not change our analysis.

Finally, Clark asks us to shift our focus from the context of L.P.'s conversation with his teachers to the jury's perception of those statements. Because, in his view, the "jury treated L.P.'s accusation as the functional equivalent of testimony," Clark argues that we must prohibit its introduction. Our Confrontation Clause decisions, however, do not determine whether a statement is testimonial by examining whether a jury would view the statement as the equivalent of in-court testimony. The logic of this argument, moreover, would lead to the conclusion that virtually all out-of-court statements offered by the prosecution are testimonial. The prosecution is unlikely to offer out-of-court statements unless they tend to support the defendant's guilt, and all such statements could be viewed as a substitute for in-court testimony. We have never suggested, however, that the Confrontation Clause bars the introduction of all out-of-court statements that support the prosecution's case. Instead, we ask whether a statement was given with the "primary purpose of creating an out-of-court substitute for trial testimony." Here, the answer is clear: L.P.'s statements to his teachers were not testimonial.

SCALIA, J., concurring in the judgment.*

[I write separately] to protest the Court's shoveling of fresh dirt upon the Sixth Amendment right of confrontation so recently rescued from the grave in Crawford v. Washington. For several decades before that case, we had been allowing hearsay statements to be admitted against a criminal defendant if they bore "indicia of reliability." Ohio v. Roberts, 448 U.S. 56 (1980). Prosecutors, past and present, love that flabby test. *Crawford* sought to bring our application of the Confrontation Clause back to its original meaning, which was to exclude unconfronted statements made by *witnesses—i.e.,* statements that were *testimonial*. We defined testimony as a "solemn declaration or affirmation made for the purpose of establishing or proving some fact"—in the context of the Confrontation Clause, a fact "potentially relevant to later criminal prosecution."

Crawford remains the law. But when else has the categorical overruling, the thorough repudiation, of an earlier line of cases been described as nothing more than "adopting a different approach"—as though *Crawford* is only a matter of twiddle-dum twiddle-dee preference, and the old, pre-*Crawford* "approach" remains available? The author unabashedly displays his hostility to *Crawford* and its progeny, perhaps aggravated by inability to muster the votes to overrule them. . . .

But snide detractions do no harm; they are just indications of motive. Dicta on legal points, however, can do harm, because though they are not binding they can mislead. Take, for example, the opinion's statement that the primary-purpose test is merely *one* of several heretofore unmentioned conditions ("necessary, but not always sufficient") that must be satisfied before the Clause's protections apply.

---

* [Justice Ginsburg joined this opinion—EDS.]

That is absolutely false, and has no support in our opinions. The Confrontation Clause categorically entitles a defendant *to be confronted with the witnesses against him*; and the primary-purpose test sorts out, among the many people who interact with the police informally, *who is acting as a witness and who is not*. Those who fall into the former category bear testimony, and are therefore acting as "witnesses," subject to the right of confrontation. There are no other mysterious requirements that the Court declines to name.

The opinion asserts that future defendants, and future Confrontation Clause majorities, must provide "evidence that the adoption of the Confrontation Clause was understood to require the exclusion of evidence that was regularly admitted in criminal cases at the time of the founding." This dictum gets the burden precisely backwards—which is of course precisely the idea. Defendants may invoke their Confrontation Clause rights once they have established that the state seeks to introduce testimonial evidence against them in a criminal case without unavailability of the witness and a previous opportunity to cross-examine. The burden is upon the prosecutor who seeks to introduce evidence *over* this bar to prove a long-established practice of introducing *specific* kinds of evidence, such as dying declarations, for which cross-examination was not typically necessary. A suspicious mind (or even one that is merely not naïve) might regard this distortion as the first step in an attempt to smuggle longstanding hearsay exceptions back into the Confrontation Clause—in other words, an attempt to return to Ohio v. Roberts.

But the good news is that there are evidently not the votes to return to that halcyon era for prosecutors; and that dicta, even calculated dicta, are nothing but dicta. They are enough, however, combined with the peculiar phenomenon of a Supreme Court opinion's aggressive hostility to precedent that it purports to be applying, to prevent my joining the writing for the Court. I concur only in the judgment.

THOMAS, J., concurring in the judgment.

. . . In the decade since we first sought to return to the original meaning of the Confrontation Clause we have carefully reserved consideration of that Clause's application to statements made to private persons for a case in which it was squarely presented. This is that case; yet the majority does not offer clear guidance on the subject, declaring only that "the primary purpose test is a necessary, but not always sufficient, condition" for a statement to fall within the scope of the Confrontation Clause. The primary purpose test, however, is just as much "an exercise in fiction . . . disconnected from history" for statements made to private persons as it is for statements made to agents of law enforcement, if not more so. I would not apply it here. Nor would I leave the resolution of this important question in doubt.

Instead, I would use the same test for statements to private persons that I have employed for statements to agents of law enforcement, assessing whether those statements bear sufficient indicia of solemnity to qualify as testimonial. This test is grounded in the history of the common-law right to confrontation, which "developed to target particular practices that occurred under the English bail and committal statutes passed during the reign of Queen Mary, namely, the civil-law mode of criminal procedure, and particularly its use of *ex parte* examinations as evidence against the accused." Reading the Confrontation Clause in light of this history, we have interpreted the accused's right to confront "the witnesses against him," U.S. Const., Amdt. 6, as the right to confront those who "bear testimony" against him. And because [testimony is] a "solemn declaration or affirmation made for the purpose of establishing or proving some fact," an analysis of statements under the Clause must turn in part on their solemnity.

I have identified several categories of extrajudicial statements that bear sufficient indicia of solemnity to fall within the original meaning of testimony. Statements "contained in formalized testimonial materials, such as affidavits, depositions, prior testimony, or confessions" easily qualify. And statements not contained in such materials may still qualify if they were obtained in "a formalized dialogue"; after the issuance of the warnings required by Miranda v. Arizona; while in police custody; or in an attempt to evade confrontation. That several of these factors seem inherently inapplicable to statements made to private persons does not mean that the test is unsuitable for analyzing such statements. All it means is that statements made to private persons rarely resemble the historical abuses that the common-law right to confrontation developed to address, and it is those practices that the test is designed to identify.

Here, L.P.'s statements do not bear sufficient indicia of solemnity to qualify as testimonial. They were neither contained in formalized testimonial materials nor obtained as the result of a formalized dialogue initiated by police. Instead, they were elicited during questioning by

L.P.'s teachers at his preschool. Nor is there any indication that L.P.'s statements were offered at trial to evade confrontation. To the contrary, the record suggests that the prosecution would have produced L.P. to testify had he been deemed competent to do so. His statements bear no "resemblance to the historical practices that the Confrontation Clause aimed to eliminate." The admission of L.P.'s extrajudicial statements thus does not implicate the Confrontation Clause. . . .

C. Self-Incrimination Privilege at Trial

Page 1330. Insert the following material at the end of note 2.

For a summary of past empirical studies of the impact of a defendant's silence on jury behavior, and a description of new experimental evidence, see Jeffrey Bellin, The Silence Penalty, 103 Iowa L. Rev. ___ (2017) (penalty defendants suffer when they refuse to testify is substantial, rivaling the more widely-recognized damage done to a defendant's trial prospects by the introduction of a criminal record).

D. Ethics and Lies at Trial

Page 1343. Insert the following material at the end of note 3.

4. *Client control over admissions of guilt*. Just as the client ultimately decides whether to testify in his or her own defense, the client controls whether or not to contest guilt. See McCoy v. Louisiana, 138 S. Ct. 1500 (2018) (Sixth Amendment guarantees a defendant the right to choose the objective of his defense and to insist that his counsel refrain from admitting guilt during jury trial, even when counsel's professional opinion is that confessing guilt offers the defendant the best chance to avoid the death penalty.

Chapter 19

Sentencing

C. *Revisiting Pleas and Trials*

1. Revisiting Proof at Trial

Page 1403. Insert this material at the end of note 3.

See also Montana v. Betterman, 136 S. Ct. 1609 (2016) (speedy trial guarantee protects the accused from arrest or indictment through trial, but does not apply once a defendant is found guilty at trial or pleads guilty to criminal charges).

D. *New Information About the Offender and the Victim*

1. Offender Information

Page 1417. Insert this material after note 5.

6. *Durability of criminal record.* Some state guidelines instruct judges to ignore prior convictions after a designated number of years, when they become "stale." Others make no distinctions between recent

convictions and older ones. For discussions of the many ways that prior criminal record influences later defendant contacts with criminal justice, see Richard S. Frase, Julian Roberts, Rhys Hester, and Kelly Mitchell, Criminal History Enhancements Sourcebook (2015); James B. Jacobs, The Eternal Criminal Record (2015).

E. Race and Sentencing

1. Race and the Victims of Crime

Page 1438. Insert this material after note 3.

4. *Hate crimes*. The substantive criminal code in many jurisdictions directly addresses the race of the victim by increasing penalties for "hate crimes," or crimes motivated in part by the race of the victim. For an in-depth treatment of the subject, see James B. Jacobs and Kimberly Potter, Hate Crimes: Criminal Law and Identity Politics (2000).

Chapter 20

Appeals

A. Who Appeals?

Page 1451. Insert this material at the end of note 2.

See Class v. United States, 138 S. Ct. 798 (2018) (guilty plea, by itself, does not bar a federal criminal defendant from challenging the constitutionality of the statute of conviction on direct appeal).

B. Appellate Review of Factual Findings

Page 1475. Insert this material at the end of note 1.

See also United States v. Musacchio, 136 S. Ct. 709 (2016) (when a jury instruction sets forth all the elements of the charged crime, but incorrectly adds one more element, a sufficiency challenge should be assessed against the correct statutory elements of the charged crime).

C. Harmless Error

Page 1487. Insert this material before Problem 20-2.

Kentel Weaver v. Massachusetts
137 S. Ct. 1899 (2017)

KENNEDY, J.*

During petitioner's trial on state criminal charges, the courtroom was occupied by potential jurors and closed to the public for two days of the jury selection process. Defense counsel neither objected to the closure at trial nor raised the issue on direct review. And the case comes to the Court on the assumption that, in failing to object, defense counsel provided ineffective assistance.

In the direct review context, the underlying constitutional violation—the courtroom closure—has been treated by this Court as a structural error, i.e., an error entitling the defendant to automatic reversal without any inquiry into prejudice. The question is whether invalidation of the conviction is required here as well, or if the prejudice inquiry is altered when the structural error is raised in the context of an ineffective-assistance-of-counsel claim.

I.

In 2003, a 15-year-old boy was shot and killed in Boston. A witness saw a young man fleeing the scene of the crime and saw him pull out a pistol. A baseball hat fell off of his head. The police recovered the hat, which featured a distinctive airbrushed Detroit Tigers logo on either side. The hat's distinctive markings linked it to 16-year-old Kentel Weaver. He is the petitioner here. DNA obtained from the hat matched petitioner's DNA.

Two weeks after the crime, the police went to petitioner's house to question him. He admitted losing his hat around the time of the shooting but denied being involved. Petitioner's mother was not so sure. Later, she questioned petitioner herself. She asked whether he had been at the scene of the shooting, and he said he had been there. But when she asked if he

* [Chief Justice Roberts and Justices Thomas, Ginsburg, Sotomayor, and Gorsuch joined this opinion—EDS.]

was the shooter, or if he knew who the shooter was, petitioner put his head down and said nothing. Believing his response to be an admission of guilt, she insisted that petitioner go to the police station to confess. He did. Petitioner was indicted in Massachusetts state court for first-degree murder and the unlicensed possession of a handgun. He pleaded not guilty and proceeded to trial.

The pool of potential jury members was large, some 60 to 100 people. The assigned courtroom could accommodate only 50 or 60 in the courtroom seating. As a result, the trial judge brought all potential jurors into the courtroom so that he could introduce the case and ask certain preliminary questions of the entire venire panel. Many of the potential jurors did not have seats and had to stand in the courtroom. After the preliminary questions, the potential jurors who had been standing were moved outside the courtroom to wait during the individual questioning of the other potential jurors. The judge acknowledged that the hallway was not "the most comfortable place to wait" and thanked the potential jurors for their patience. The judge noted that there was simply not space in the courtroom for everybody.

As all of the seats in the courtroom were occupied by the venire panel, an officer of the court excluded from the courtroom any member of the public who was not a potential juror. So when petitioner's mother and her minister came to the courtroom to observe the two days of jury selection, they were turned away.

All this occurred before the Court's decision in Presley v. Georgia, 558 U.S. 209 (2010). *Presley* made it clear that the public-trial right extends to jury selection as well as to other portions of the trial. Before *Presley*, Massachusetts courts would often close courtrooms to the public during jury selection, in particular during murder trials.

In this case petitioner's mother told defense counsel about the closure at some point during jury selection. But counsel "believed that a courtroom closure for [jury selection] was constitutional." As a result, he "did not discuss the matter" with petitioner, or tell him that his right to a public trial included the jury voir dire, or object to the closure.

During the ensuing trial, the government presented strong evidence of petitioner's guilt. Its case consisted of the incriminating details outlined above, including petitioner's confession to the police. The jury convicted petitioner on both counts. The court sentenced him to life in prison on the murder charge and to about a year in prison on the gun-possession charge.

Five years later, petitioner filed a motion for a new trial in Massachusetts state court. As relevant here, he argued that his attorney had provided ineffective assistance by failing to object to the courtroom closure. After an evidentiary hearing, the trial court recognized a violation of the right to a public trial based on the following findings: The courtroom had been closed; the closure was neither de minimis nor trivial; the closure was unjustified; and the closure was full rather than partial (meaning that all members of the public, rather than only some of them, had been excluded from the courtroom). The trial court further determined that defense counsel failed to object because of "serious incompetency, inefficiency, or inattention." On the other hand, petitioner had not "offered any evidence or legal argument establishing prejudice." For that reason, the court held that petitioner was not entitled to relief.

Petitioner appealed the denial of the motion for a new trial to the Massachusetts Supreme Judicial Court. The court consolidated that appeal with petitioner's direct appeal. As noted, there had been no objection to the closure at trial; and the issue was not raised in the direct appeal. The Supreme Judicial Court then affirmed in relevant part. Although it recognized that a violation of the Sixth Amendment right to a public trial constitutes "structural error," the court stated that petitioner had "failed to show that trial counsel's conduct caused prejudice warranting a new trial." On this reasoning, the court rejected petitioner's claim of ineffective assistance of counsel.

There is disagreement among the Federal Courts of Appeals and some state courts of last resort about whether a defendant must demonstrate prejudice in a case like this one—in which a structural error is neither preserved nor raised on direct review but is raised later via a claim alleging ineffective assistance of counsel. . . .

II.

This case requires a discussion, and the proper application, of two doctrines: structural error and ineffective assistance of counsel. The two doctrines are intertwined; for the reasons an error is deemed structural may influence the proper standard used to evaluate an ineffective-assistance claim premised on the failure to object to that error.

A.

The concept of structural error can be discussed first. In Chapman v. California, 386 U.S. 18 (1967), this Court adopted the general rule that a constitutional error does not automatically require reversal of a conviction. If the government can show beyond a reasonable doubt that the error complained of did not contribute to the verdict obtained, the Court held, then the error is deemed harmless and the defendant is not entitled to reversal.

The Court recognized, however, that some errors should not be deemed harmless beyond a reasonable doubt. These errors came to be known as structural errors. The purpose of the structural error doctrine is to ensure insistence on certain basic, constitutional guarantees that should define the framework of any criminal trial. Thus, the defining feature of a structural error is that it affects the "framework within which the trial proceeds," rather than being "simply an error in the trial process itself." For the same reason, a structural error defies analysis by harmless error standards.

The precise reason why a particular error is not amenable to that kind of analysis—and thus the precise reason why the Court has deemed it structural—varies in a significant way from error to error. There appear to be at least three broad rationales.

First, an error has been deemed structural in some instances if the right at issue is not designed to protect the defendant from erroneous conviction but instead protects some other interest. This is true of the defendant's right to conduct his own defense, which, when exercised, "usually increases the likelihood of a trial outcome unfavorable to the defendant." McKaskle v. Wiggins, 465 U.S. 168 (1984). That right is based on the fundamental legal principle that a defendant must be allowed to make his own choices about the proper way to protect his own liberty. See Faretta v. California, 422 U.S. 806 (1975). Because harm is irrelevant to the basis underlying the right, the Court has deemed a violation of that right structural error. See United States v. Gonzalez-Lopez, 548 U.S. 140 (2006).

Second, an error has been deemed structural if the effects of the error are simply too hard to measure. For example, when a defendant is denied the right to select his or her own attorney, the precise "effect of the violation cannot be ascertained." Because the government will, as a result, find it almost impossible to show that the error was "harmless beyond a reasonable doubt," the efficiency costs of letting the government try to make the showing are unjustified.

Third, an error has been deemed structural if the error always results in fundamental unfairness. For example, if an indigent defendant is denied an attorney or if the judge fails to give a reasonable-doubt instruction, the resulting trial is always a fundamentally unfair one. See Gideon v. Wainwright, 372 U.S. 335 (1963) (right to an attorney); Sullivan v. Louisiana, 508 U.S. 275 (1993) (right to a reasonable-doubt instruction). It therefore would be futile for the government to try to show harmlessness.

These categories are not rigid. In a particular case, more than one of these rationales may be part of the explanation for why an error is deemed to be structural. For these purposes, however, one point is critical: An error can count as structural even if the error does not lead to fundamental unfairness in every case.

B.

As noted above, a violation of the right to a public trial is a structural error. It is relevant to determine why that is so. In particular, the question is whether a public-trial violation counts as structural because it always leads to fundamental unfairness or for some other reason.

In Waller v. Georgia, 467 U.S. 39 (1984), the state court prohibited the public from viewing a weeklong suppression hearing out of concern for the privacy of persons other than those on trial. Although it recognized that there would be instances where closure was justified, this Court noted that "such circumstances will be rare" and that the closure in question was unjustified. Still, the Court did not order a new trial. Instead it ordered a new suppression hearing that was open to the public. If the same evidence was found admissible in that renewed pretrial proceeding, the Court held, no new trial as to guilt would be necessary. This was despite the structural aspect of the violation.

Some 25 years after the *Waller* decision, the Court issued its per curiam ruling in Presley v. Georgia. In that case, as here, the courtroom was closed to the public during jury voir dire. Unlike here, however, there was a trial objection to the closure, and the issue was raised on direct appeal. On review of the State Supreme Court's decision allowing the closure, this Court expressed concern that the state court's reasoning would allow the courtroom to be closed during jury selection "whenever the trial judge decides, for whatever reason, that he or she would prefer to fill the courtroom with potential jurors rather than spectators." Although the Court expressly noted that courtroom closure may be ordered in some circumstances, the Court also stated that it was "still incumbent upon" the trial court "to consider all reasonable alternatives to closure."

These opinions teach that courtroom closure is to be avoided, but that there are some circumstances when it is justified. The problems that may be encountered by trial courts in deciding whether some closures are necessary, or even in deciding which members of the public should be admitted when seats are scarce, are difficult ones. For example, there are often preliminary instructions that a judge may want to give to the venire as a whole, rather than repeating those instructions (perhaps with unintentional differences) to several groups of potential jurors. On the other hand, various constituencies of the public—the family of the accused, the family of the victim, members of the press, and other persons—all have their own interests in observing the selection of jurors. How best to manage these problems is not a topic discussed at length in any decision or commentary the Court has found.

So although the public-trial right is structural, it is subject to exceptions. See Simonson, The Criminal Court Audience in a Post-Trial World, 127 Harv. L. Rev. 2173 (2014) (discussing situations in which a trial court may order a courtroom closure). Though these cases should be rare, a judge may deprive a defendant of his right to an open courtroom by making proper factual findings in support of the decision to do so. The fact that the public-trial right is subject to these exceptions suggests that not every public-trial violation results in fundamental unfairness. . . .

III.

The Court now turns to the proper remedy for addressing the violation of a structural right, and in particular the right to a public trial. [We must decide] what showing is necessary when the defendant does not preserve a structural error on direct review but raises it later in the context of an ineffective-assistance-of-counsel claim. To obtain relief on the basis of ineffective assistance of counsel, the defendant as a general rule bears the burden to meet two standards. First, the defendant must show deficient performance—that the attorney's error was "so serious that counsel was not functioning as the 'counsel' guaranteed the defendant by the Sixth Amendment." Strickland v. Washington, 466 U.S. 668 (1984). Second, the defendant must show that the attorney's error "prejudiced the defense."

The prejudice showing is in most cases a necessary part of a *Strickland* claim. The reason is that a defendant has a right to effective representation, not a right to an attorney who performs his duties "mistake-free." As a rule, therefore, a "violation of the Sixth Amendment right to effective representation is not 'complete' until the defendant is prejudiced."

That said, the concept of prejudice is defined in different ways depending on the context in which it appears. In the ordinary *Strickland* case, prejudice means "a reasonable probability that, but for counsel's unprofessional errors, the result of the proceeding would have been different." But the *Strickland* Court cautioned that the prejudice inquiry is not meant to be applied in a "mechanical" fashion. For when a court is evaluating an ineffective-assistance claim, the ultimate inquiry must concentrate on "the fundamental fairness of the proceeding." Petitioner therefore argues that under a proper interpretation of *Strickland*, even if there is no showing of a reasonable probability of a different outcome, relief still must be granted if the convicted person shows that attorney errors rendered the trial fundamentally unfair. For the analytical purposes of this case, the Court will assume that petitioner's interpretation of *Strickland* is the correct one. In light of the Court's ultimate holding, however, the Court need not decide that question here.

As explained above, not every public-trial violation will in fact lead to a fundamentally unfair trial. Nor can it be said that the failure to object to a public-trial violation always deprives the defendant of a reasonable probability of a different outcome. Thus, when a defendant raises a public-trial violation via an ineffective-assistance-of-counsel claim, *Strickland* prejudice is not shown automatically. Instead, the burden is on the defendant to show either a reasonable probability of a different outcome in his or her case or, as the Court has assumed for these purposes, to show that the particular public-trial violation was so serious as to render his or her trial fundamentally unfair. . . .

The reason for placing the burden on the petitioner in this case . . . derives both from the nature of the error, and the difference between a public-trial violation preserved and then raised on direct review and a public-trial violation raised as an ineffective-assistance-of-counsel claim. As explained above, when a defendant objects to a courtroom closure, the trial court can either order the courtroom opened or explain the reasons for keeping it closed. When a defendant first raises the closure in an ineffective-assistance claim, however, the trial court is deprived of the chance to cure the violation either by opening the courtroom or by explaining the reasons for closure.

Furthermore, when state or federal courts adjudicate errors objected to during trial and then raised on direct review, the systemic costs of remedying the error are diminished to some extent. That is because, if a new trial is ordered on direct review, there may be a reasonable chance that not too much time will have elapsed for witness memories still to be accurate and physical evidence not to be lost. There are also advantages of direct judicial supervision. Reviewing courts, in the regular course of the appellate process, can give instruction to the trial courts in a familiar context that allows for elaboration of the relevant principles based on review of an adequate record. For instance, in this case, the factors and circumstances that might justify a temporary closure are best considered in the regular appellate process and not in the context of a later proceeding, with its added time delays.

When an ineffective-assistance-of-counsel claim is raised in postconviction proceedings, the costs and uncertainties of a new trial are greater because more time will have elapsed in most cases. The finality interest is more at risk, and direct review often has given at least one opportunity for an appellate review of trial proceedings. These differences justify a different standard for evaluating a structural error depending on whether it is raised on direct review or raised instead in a claim alleging ineffective assistance of counsel. . . .

IV.

The final inquiry concerns the ineffective-assistance claim in this case. Although the case comes on the assumption that petitioner has shown deficient performance by counsel, he has not shown prejudice in the ordinary sense, i.e., a reasonable probability that the jury would not have convicted him if his attorney had objected to the closure.

It is of course possible that potential jurors might have behaved differently if petitioner's family had been present. And it is true that the presence of the public might have had some bearing on juror reaction. But here petitioner offered no evidence or legal argument establishing prejudice in the sense of a reasonable probability of a different outcome but for counsel's failure to object.

In other circumstances a different result might obtain. If, for instance, defense counsel errs in failing to object when the government's main witness testifies in secret, then the defendant might be able to show prejudice with little more detail. Even in those circumstances, however, the burden would remain on the defendant to make the prejudice showing, because a public-trial violation does not always lead to a fundamentally unfair trial.

In light of the above assumption that prejudice can be shown by a demonstration of fundamental unfairness, the remaining question is whether petitioner has shown that counsel's failure to object rendered the trial fundamentally unfair. The Court concludes that petitioner has not made the showing. Although petitioner's mother and her minister were indeed excluded from the courtroom for two days during jury selection, petitioner's trial was not conducted in secret or in a remote place. Cf. In re Oliver, 333 U.S. 257 (1948). The closure was limited to the jury voir dire; the courtroom remained open during the evidentiary phase of the trial; the closure decision apparently was made by court officers rather than the judge; there were many members of the venire who did not become jurors but who did observe the proceedings; and there was a record made of the proceedings that does not indicate any basis for concern, other than the closure itself.

There has been no showing, furthermore, that the potential harms flowing from a courtroom closure came to pass in this case. For example, there is no suggestion that any juror lied during voir dire; no suggestion of misbehavior by the prosecutor, judge, or any other party; and no suggestion that any of the participants failed to approach their duties with the neutrality and serious purpose that our system demands. . . .

In sum, petitioner has not shown a reasonable probability of a different outcome but for counsel's failure to object, and he has not shown that counsel's shortcomings led to a fundamentally unfair trial. He is not entitled to a new trial.

In the criminal justice system, the constant, indeed unending, duty of the judiciary is to seek and to find the proper balance between the necessity for fair and just trials and the importance of finality of judgments. When a structural error is preserved and raised on direct review, the balance is in the defendant's favor, and a new trial generally will be granted as a matter of right. When a structural error is raised in the context of an ineffective-assistance claim, however, finality concerns are far more pronounced. For this reason, and in light of the other circumstances present in this case, petitioner must show prejudice in order to obtain a new trial. As explained above, he has not made the required showing. The judgment of the Massachusetts Supreme Judicial Court is affirmed.

BREYER, J., dissenting.*

The Court notes that *Strickland*'s prejudice inquiry is not meant to be applied in a mechanical fashion, and I agree. But, in my view, it follows from this principle that a defendant who shows that his attorney's constitutionally deficient performance produced a structural error should not face the additional—and often insurmountable—*Strickland* hurdle of demonstrating that the error changed the outcome of his proceeding. . . .

The Court has recognized that structural errors' distinctive attributes make them defy analysis by harmless-error standards. It has therefore categorically exempted structural errors from the case-by-case harmlessness review to which trial errors are subjected. Our precedent does not try to parse which structural errors are the truly egregious ones. It simply views all structural errors as "intrinsically harmful" and holds that any structural error warrants automatic reversal on direct appeal without regard to its effect on the outcome of a trial.

The majority here does not take this approach. It assumes that some structural errors—those that "lead to fundamental unfairness"—but not others, can warrant relief without a showing of actual prejudice under *Strickland*. While I agree that a showing of fundamental unfairness is sufficient to satisfy *Strickland*, I would not try to draw this distinction.
Even if some structural errors do not create fundamental unfairness, all structural errors nonetheless have features that make them "defy analysis by 'harmless-error' standards." This is why all structural errors—not just the "fundamental unfairness" ones—are exempt from harmlessness inquiry and warrant automatic reversal on direct review. Those same features mean that all structural errors defy an actual-prejudice analysis under *Strickland*. . . .

---

* [Justice Kagan joined this opinion—EDS.]

In my view, we should not require defendants to take on a task that is normally impossible to perform. Nor would I give lower courts the unenviably complex job of deciphering which structural errors really undermine fundamental fairness and which do not—that game is not worth the candle. I would simply say that just as structural errors are categorically insusceptible to harmless-error analysis on direct review, so too are they categorically insusceptible to actual-prejudice analysis in *Strickland* claims. A showing that an attorney's constitutionally deficient performance produced a structural error should consequently be enough to entitle a defendant to relief. I respectfully dissent.

D. Retroactivity

Page 1496. Insert this material at the end of note 1.

See also State v. Mares 335 P.3d 487 (Wyo. 2014) (constitutional ban on mandatory juvenile sentences of life without parole applies retroactively to cases not final at time of Supreme Court ruling; surveys split of authority).

Page 1497. Insert this material at the end of note 3.

See Davila v. Davis, 137 S. Ct. 2058 (2017) (defendant cannot not obtain federal habeas corpus relief based on a substantial but procedurally defaulted claim of ineffective assistant of state postconviction counsel).